James Willstrop was born in Norfolk in 1983 before moving to Yorkshire. He is a former world junior champion, became world No 1 in the January 2012 rankings and has won over 80 caps for England. He writes a regular column for the *Yorkshire Evening Post*.

D0888805

First Printed, 2012

ISBN: 978-0-9571391-0-7

Cover design: Ed Way, spraydesigns.co.uk
Front and back cover images: Steve Line / Squashpics.com

For more information on authors:
James Willstrop
www.willstrop.co.uk
Rod Gilmour
www.gilmourmedia.com

Printed and bound in Great Britain by
CPI Group (UK) Ltd, Croydon, Surrey CR0 4YY

Shot and a Ghost

A year in the brutal world of professional squash

CAST OF CHARACTERS

Malcolm (Malc) Willstrop – father, coach.

Vanessa Atkinson – girlfriend, former world champion and world No 1.

David Campion – half-brother, coach and England Squash assistant national coach.

Mick Todd – Pontefract Squash Club owner, and my manager.

Nick Matthew – Yorkshireman who became world No 1 in 2010. Double world and Commonwealth champion.

Ramy Ashour – Egypt's young sensation. A revelation with a racket in his hands. He has to be seen to be believed.

Pontefract Squash and Leisure Club – Yorkshire club with a healthy junior programme where I learnt my trade.

PREFACE

Literature has long been a source of fascination to me. Deep down, I have always harboured ambitions of writing a book. Sitting here now, having actually finished it, before my squash career has even ended, is a sobering thought.

It was at breakfast one morning at the Kuwait World Open in November 2009 that *The Daily Telegraph*'s Rod Gilmour mentioned the idea of writing a diary over the year, having read my *Yorkshire Evening Post* columns.

I was keen and met him at the Tournament of Champions in New York in 2010. If it were to be written in my name, then I wanted to write the book myself, a huge undertaking (just how big, I had little idea) rather than have it ghostwritten. Today's bookshelves are rife with prematurely written autobiographies about the rich and famous. As I am neither, my motives for writing a book are rather different.

I was quite sure that people wouldn't want to read much about my formative years frolicking around naked in Uncle Mike and Aunt Julie's paddling pool. Instead I resolved to limit the content to the topics I felt would really interest people: what it feels like to play a World Open final, the pain of a hard training session, or a response to the loss of a special person.

I found myself naturally drawn to including flashbacks to give the narrative some context. My mother, Lesley's death in 2000 was devastating and it was a natural reaction to write about her and my memories with her. She features prominently and I hope that the excerpts I have included give balance to the book. It is safe to say I withheld nothing of my feelings regarding her decline, or anything else for that matter.

I may regret being so candid about so private a matter, but it felt right at the time, and it was an immensely cathartic process that, in hindsight, I would have benefited from years ago. Many of us hide behind masks, which cover all the insecurities, doubts and even delights of our lives. I, like many, tend not to show outward emotion but find it much easier to write honestly.

We all deal with the trivialities of life from day-to-day, whether it be playing squash, working or socialising, but there are always times when we have more significant matters to deal with: failure, a sudden parting of ways, or death – the ultimate parting. I didn't see the point of continuing a project of this kind if it didn't convey raw truth and integrity.

Rod and I agreed that, with his experience, he would be ideally placed to scrutinise and edit my work and I would like to thank him for helping me to realise this long-held ambition, and for giving great commitment to this project. His has been a serious effort.

PROLOGUE

11 February 2011

**British National Championships quarter-finals.
Sportcity, Manchester.**

'Match to Kemp. 11-7, 11-6, 10-12, 11-8.'

The crowd applauds the result, reacting enthusiastically to the compère. Quite rightly, Jonathan Kemp's surprising but deserved win over me is lauded.

I come off court and slump in my chair. My head is in my hands. My dad Malcolm stands by, not quite knowing how best to approach the situation. He recognises there is more going on in my head than just losing a squash match. I don't enjoy it any more and I'm genuinely glad I don't have to play in the semis. During the intervals Malcolm asked me to hang in there. The only reply I could muster was: 'Why should I when I don't actually care?'

Not long ago, neither of us could ever have imagined such a phrase escaping my mouth. Squash has always been such a positive part of my life. I remember coming to the Nationals and the British Open as a kid and dreaming about one day walking onto this stage to play. I would talk endlessly to my parents about being a top squash player.

During the school holidays I regularly surfaced at the crack of dawn to watch footage of Pakistan greats Jahangir and Jansher Khan, Canadian magician Jonathon Power and Britain's former world No 1 Peter Nicol, any videos I could get my hands on. Yet here I am, on the big stage, my perspective clouded and contorted.

Too many matches, too many flights, not enough training, not enough rest. It is hardly surprising that it has come to this.

Children come for autographs and a few friends come down to my corner. I can hardly find it in myself to respond. I can't get out of Manchester fast enough. But not before the press arrive. They have to kneel as I'm sitting on the floor against a wall behind the court. And it's clear to them that I want to pour my heart out. Shattered physically but even more so mentally, I am on the verge of a complete breakdown. I say exactly how I am feeling.

'I've had enough – I'm just not enjoying playing at the moment.

'There's no point in carrying on like this – maybe I need to stop playing for a while.

'It's unnatural for me not to like playing. The only reason I'm putting the effort in is to do justice to all the people who have come to watch me play.'

Three days later I'm back playing.

ONE

STARTING WITH A BANG

28 January 2010

**Grand Hyatt, 42nd and Lexington, NYC, Room 3067.
5:30am.**

The room is black. I twist and turn and plead with myself
to fall asleep. Why is sleep always so difficult? Some say a
conscience inhibits sleep, and maybe they are right. I am
left with my thoughts. A sudden jolt, like electricity, runs
through my body as I remember that I am playing tonight
at the best squash venue in the world, Grand Central
Terminus in New York, against Ramy Ashour, Egypt's star
and one of the finest players to ever hold a racket. It's the
Tournament of Champions final. I wonder if there is ever a
day when an athlete ceases to feel this excitement ahead of
competition. Perhaps when he does, then it is time to give
up.

I sense excitement upon waking but it is quickly
eradicated by a horrible counterblow, a feeling of doubt I
know all too well. I remember I jarred my ankle during the
previous day's match: the same ankle on which I had
surgery last April. I wiggle it in bed. No chance of sleep
now, it's the ankle and it's stiff. Please no, not again. Let me
not have done it again. All that work and time, and just as I
was beginning to forget, could it have come back to niggle
away in my head? Doubt, doubt, doubt.

I could ring Ali, my physio back home, as it's the middle
of the day there. Or I could take a sleeping pill so that I can
catch another few hours' sleep. I consider this mini-
conundrum and then decide against both.

I suddenly remember that I haven't written my column

for the *Yorkshire Evening Post*. It's no problem, I'm awake anyway, need something to do to occupy the time, and I haven't missed the deadline. I take my computer out and reel off 400 words in no time. Result. That's that done.

I still can't sleep, and so I lie there thinking about tonight. I feel terribly fortunate to be able to go out into one of the great iconic venues of the world and play, battle, and try to beat somebody. It's a circus, but what a thing to be able to wake up and do. I think of all the awful jobs people undertake, and then I consider the fascinating homeless characters in Grand Central, and the day that they face. I feel fortunate.

I stumble to the window of my hotel room, preposterously doing a kind of test movement on my ankle, almost like a lunge. I say out loud: 'What are you doing, you clown?' and I realise that there is no way I would have done this had I not been alone. I open the window and invite New York in. Taxi horns bellow and tell me indirectly of people's troubles. An ambulance siren announces itself to midtown's constant and always changing flurry of people, who rush like ants and dart and dodge to temporary destinations. New York has the ability to make one feel so alive, yet there are reminders of the harsher side of life. It is a side of life even the most wondrous city can't hide.

It's 7:45am. I give up on sleep and ring my dad, Malc. I know he'll be up. 'Not sleeping. Early breakfast?' I inquire. 'See you in five minutes.'

I look forward to breakfast with Malc, partly because I like eating, but also because I enjoy his company. People have all sorts of ideas about him; he is controversial, a one off, but he is mostly enormous fun as far as I'm concerned. There is an image he projects to people on the outside which contrasts to the character I work with on a day-to-day basis. People have ideas about him locking me in a cell if I don't win, and if anyone suggests it to be so then I tend to promote the idea for laughs.

If anything I am the critical piece in the jigsaw, and he is the one who lends a logical and sensible point of view if I am found lacking. I gather my additionals (soy milk, coffee replacement stuff, porridge toppings) and meet him in the lobby. We talk about anything, and there is a palpable tone of excitement in his voice which tells me that a day like this is about his life's work, not just mine.

Malc can't be everywhere, at every tournament with me. Squash players – Malc has been a coach for over 50 years and played at county level – haven't the financial capacity to cart their coaches about as golfers and tennis players do. He endures the disappointments and enjoys the success as much as I do, so to have at least made a final with him here is very special.

At noon I meet with England coaches Stafford Murray and David Pearson to look at the stats on wonder kid Ramy. It doesn't get complicated but it clears one or two things up in my head, offering facts rather than speculation. Stafford relays the information to me: where Ramy makes his errors, where he hits the most of his winners and how he responds to a certain length of rally. Stafford has the videos to back his facts and we watch one or two clips. Malcolm, David and I then discuss with Stafford a plan of sorts. This collective discussion between two world-class coaches, a world-class player and an experienced performance analyst encapsulates perfectly what world-class sport is all about. There are no egos here. Each person in that room wants one result, and that is for me to win tonight. Each party is willing to discuss and listen. I am pleased that Malcolm and David have a relationship in which they share ideas and work together, despite being very different, and this is quite rare amongst top-class coaches.

Closing in on match time, I find I can do nothing that demands any deep or challenging thought. I struggle to read, so I stick to the TV. *Everybody Loves Raymond* will do for now. Until the adverts come on that is. Advertising on television in the States is a disaster. Not only do the adverts interrupt programmes painfully often, but they are tacky and so litigation obsessed it is mystifying that anyone can do anything but laugh at them!

The afternoon before the match is a pressing passage of time, when the brain is less occupied, and as it gets closer thoughts focus more on it. The nerves kick in. I remember playing Australian Anthony Ricketts, my close friend and training partner at the time, in the British Open final in 2005 and the overwhelming feeling was sheer terror. Even walking to the venue made my stomach sink. I spoke to him afterwards and he said he felt similarly awful that day. I learned I wasn't the only one; every player feels the pinch.

I eat, shower and talk to myself. Sport can make a person live life in such a ridiculous manner: lying about all day, not sleeping and having conversations in the shower. I think good, happy thoughts and about hitting brilliant shots. I get ready, check my stuff at least four times. Four red shirts, two shorts, socks, wristbands, bandanas. There's too much here but I make sure. Water bottles, drinks, energy gels.

I stop and think for a moment about having to take an energy gel if I hit a physical wall in two hours' time, and I shudder. Momentarily considering Ramy's bag-packing routine, I absurdly conclude that it won't be as clinical as mine: we played in Egypt in September and in between games, amid chaos on a Cairo outside court, he asked to borrow my towel as he'd forgotten his own!

My girlfriend Vanessa and I walk down through the Grand Hyatt to the shopping precinct and the rush hour buzz of Grand Central. Confronting this in itself requires a level of athletic and mental aptitude. There are swarms of people all going in different directions. We dodge and weave through the crowds. The odd person glances at my racket bag, but whilst it is slightly unusual in most railway terminals in the world, it is not here.

As we come back together we talk for something to do; she keeps me relaxed; she's been there before, winning the World Open, holding the world No 1 position. She knows the butterfly feeling rather well.

We walk towards Vanderbilt Hall where the glass court shimmers, and the people gather there behind the front wall, for the free view, like at a rock concert. Vanessa heads to the bar; she is naturally drawn to such things. Can I come too? Let's forget this squash lark, put me out of my misery and make mine a double ...

I shoot through the crowds to the warm-up area, behind the scaffolding at the back of the court. Ramy sweeps past me with his hood up over his head, storming through a back door to find some corner of a rush hour affected Grand Central Terminus to warm-up. We half nod, knowing we can rely on each other to play cleanly tonight.

The atmosphere in Grand Central is simply electric. I stand waiting to be announced and I can't believe my luck to be playing in the final here for the second time, on a sporting occasion of gargantuan proportions. I wonder how it all came to this, and briefly think about playing squash as a child at Pontefract, the club in Yorkshire where I first started to play the game. My God, these are the moments to enjoy. Peering over the stands I take a look at the crowd, waiting to be entertained under that iconic chandelier in the Beaux-Arts Vanderbilt Hall. I shiver with anticipation.

* * *

I am behind all the way in the first. The pace at which he plays always takes my breath away and requires some getting used to, but I quickly adapt and I recover to take the game 12-10. The backhand length is flowing and I'm not leaving the ball too short, which means that he gets no angles to attack. I play positively to the front court, giving him plenty to think about and me plenty to be positive about. There is little physical damage and the momentum is all mine. Malc is thrilled that I manage to steal the game after an early points deficit. He reinforces to me that containment is key, punctuated with subtle spells of consistent attack. Sounds easy.

And in the second it is. This time I control the game, winning 11-5. It is smooth, it is effortless and, as had been the case all week, it happens without me thinking. The third is the closest and most entertaining of the match, in which he reapplies the pressure, throwing the kitchen sink at me. He plays his shots with style – hurtling around the court with ease – but only wins it 12-10, a huge positive for me. If I can push him so close through his strongest spells it is a great sign. He has to reach this level twice more to win the match, knowing that my resistance shows no sign of waning.

Nevertheless my lungs and legs burn after the second interval. Two minutes is not enough rest and the lactic acid is exacting. Time for an energy gel to give me a boost, perhaps mentally more than physically. I gulp down drinks and steady myself for a big push. Malc raises his voice so that I can hear him over the noise of an inspired New York crowd. He calmly implores me to 'stick with it, and have faith.' I notice a camera in my face and hear shouting from the audience as I fret about for towels and drinks.

Before I know it the score stands 6-1 in my favour, a score indicative of a spell of play that I can only describe as 'dream squash'. I am accurate and he hits the tin. Then comes a difficult spell and I'm remembering that the man I oppose is one of the only players in the world who can hit five winners in a row in the blink of an eye. If he does that now it is 6-6, so I resolve to think about each point in turn, playing as tightly as possible without becoming edgy in attack.

For some strange reason I recall an instance when Chris Walker, the former England international, when 2-0 up against Aussie Rodney Eyles, said in an interview that he committed the 'cardinal sin' of thinking about the next round, before winning the match. How this comes in to my head I have no idea, but it does. I decide not to commit this cardinal sin and steer clear of any thoughts of winning. I close the game out 11-4 with a forehand volley. After all the hard work, it takes me a few seconds to accept another major title is finally in my hands. It's been a long time coming, since 2008 in fact. I almost lose myself right there and then but Ramy is behind me and we shake hands after which I thrust my racket and arms into the air in jubilation. It's good to hear the crowd respond.

I give the longest speech in the history of tournament speeches, but I make no apology: there are many people I feel compelled to thank, and I don't get a platform like this in which to do so every day. What is more, half of them are here, which makes it feel like the most precious of all my tournament wins. After all the many disappointments, it is wonderful to enjoy the champagne reception afterwards and at dinner we talk about the people who have doubted (a group in which I probably include myself) and criticised, the people who have said I am too nice to be a winner, or that I can't win being a vegetarian.

At about 2:30am it is time to leave. On the hotel room bed lie the trophy and the winners' cheque. Now is the time for proper reflection. I sit on the bed, wondering what on earth I do now. Kit, dirty and clean, lies strewn about. My mind is busy and remnants of adrenalin still surge through my body. There is absolutely no way I will sleep so

I settle for this curious, lonely sensation, grateful that I am feeling an emptiness having won and not lost. The post-tournament comedown has fully taken hold; I have a sore throat coming on, an imminent infection which is a result of the intensity I have maintained for several days now. I replay what happened over and over and over. I look at the clock, which says 5:30am. A little later, I finally drop off to sleep, but not for long.

31 January 2010

After opting to stay an extra day in New York we saw *West Side Story* on Broadway. Interestingly, despite his very macho image, Mick Todd, my manager, is fond of musical theatre. I was brought up on the stuff as a child; my parents took me on regular visits. I developed an obsession for *Joseph and the Amazing Technicolour Dreamcoat* by Andrew Lloyd Webber, and since my childhood have probably seen it a dozen times, also playing the part in a school play.

I still have this fascination with the theatre now, and I'm sure that is because I was so exposed to it as a child. Each time I visit New York or London, I try to go. It is unlike film as a form of entertainment; there is a magic at the theatre that is hard to capture in film. Of course, the theatre has camp connotations as a means of entertainment, but I have never been frightened of letting my feminine side in.

If most people tried the theatre or ballet, casting aside any preconceptions, they would like it, or at least appreciate it, if it was thought hip to do so. Mick and I once saw *Mamma Mia* together in London. Apart from Abba's music, it was one of the less good musicals we had seen but we sat there with all the middle-aged women. It occurred to me how incongruous this may seem, but it was natural to us. I thought back to my blissful childhood evening at

Pontefract Squash Club when I was running riot, and remembered how circumspect my feelings were towards Mick, a grunting man at the bar who drank beer with lots of other men and shouted at little children. He was different to my dad, who was well spoken and encouraged politeness and respect. In essence, Mick and myself, and perhaps my dad, are all very, very different, yet we get on famously.

I talked a lot to Mick about this at a tournament once, when he was accusing me of being overly cynical, and we mentioned our differences. He is confident and positive, I can be shy and negative. He likes pubs and blokes, I like poetry and music. He likes people, I like hotel rooms. There doesn't seem to be acres of common ground, yet the relationship we have formed recently has become warm, and he is now one of my closest pals.

6 February 2010

Had a dream last night that Vanessa and I had moved house from Leeds to a rundown neighbourhood, an awful place, and there was a cricket ground behind the main street. Malcolm, who couldn't believe we had moved there, thought we had lost our minds. Vanessa and I went in to the cricket ground where Cameron Pilley, one of the top Aussies on tour, was batting and Amr Shabana, Egypt's four-time world champion, was bowling. Pilley was hitting Shabana all over the pitch for fours and sixes but in my strange dream he was beating him 12-10, 11-4, so it was a mixture of squash and cricket. I wondered for a minute what Shabana was doing. I wouldn't have thought he would have even heard of cricket, and they certainly don't play it in Egypt. It doesn't strike me as being a game suited to the Egyptian way, and it was no surprise that an Aussie was hitting him all over the ground. No sooner had I thought that than Shabana came off retired hurt.

Not sure what to make of it all but I hoped my dreams of Shabana's downfall might ring true today as he was my opponent in the semis at the Swedish Open. The court was dead as a doornail, perfect for the shot-player (the ball stays further up the court on a deader court, making good shots even better), so I knew I would have my hands full but I had plenty of confidence in my own ability. As I had envisaged, it was a shoot-out. I saw his ears prick up in the first as the rallies were short and his attack as lethal as ever in propitious conditions for the world's greatest shot maker. However, I recovered well and played some impressive stuff. The racket was working well and there were no errors. I turned it around to win 3-1, my second win over him in two weeks. I carried the form through from New York and I now face another showdown with England No 1 Nick Matthew, a big rival and fellow Yorkshireman.

Had a chat with Malc at dinner where we broached the subject of his writing. It is an unusual situation for someone to be the foremost writer on squash and having, at the same time, to write about a relation, something that has not always sat comfortably with me I have to admit. I remember one blazing row concerning an issue in Bermuda at the breakfast table, to the horror of onlookers. Poor little James, they probably thought, with his misanthropic grump of a father, but I had my say.

Malc has a distinct way about him, a way by which it is impossible not to be enlightened or interested. If he talks, people listen; when he regales an audience, people are either amused or horrified. He divides opinion, and is sometimes teeth-clenchingly controversial, but he is always, always worth listening to. You either love him or hate him. There is little middle ground; his writing is never watered down. He says things exactly as he sees them and there is so little of this attitude in modern society that it can be fortifying to many, offensive to some.

I love to read his articles; they are informative and interesting, and very well written, but I often struggle when reading pieces he has written about me. I am aware that people think he is biased. Mick and Malcolm have had several heated conversations about this over coffee before training in the mornings. Mick thinks that there is an element of bias and he also speaks from the point of view of many others who think so in the public. I have to say that although I don't feel particularly comfortable when he writes about me, I have scoured many of his articles and whilst he can write positively about me at times, perhaps it is justified in his eyes. I am, after all, one of the best players in the world. Is it acceptable to ask him to avoid writing about me? I am also the one player who is likely to live up to the standards he most condones, having been raised and influenced by him all my life.

He is very often at the tournaments I play where we work together, and is always coaching me, and therefore will be more inclined to write about my match than what is going on the court next door.

He always comes up with solid answers to any hint of criticisms of his writings.

'I don't just praise you. Check my articles, look at what I have said about Shabana in the past. I have written full features saying how great a player he is. I said recently that Ramy was the most outrageous racket player the world has ever seen. If a father was that concerned about preserving his son's reputation then I wouldn't say that about one of his closest rivals. I say good things about Gregory Gaultier and Nick, although I have often not liked their disposition on court. So it is not just you I praise, but if I like what you do, then I'll say so.'

There have always been players Malc has not taken to, which isn't particularly remarkable because it is a trait of Malc's to not like people, but it could affect me if I have to play such an opponent. He often gets ideas about people in his mind that stick, and are unchangeable. I lose count of the number of people who come up to me and say, 'Oh your dad's not talking to me, has he got a problem with me?'

'Probably not', I reply. 'He doesn't like many people, so I wouldn't worry yourself. Just ignore him! Then he might respond.'

He doesn't feel he has to talk to people and can appear rude to many, which is ironic considering he is hell bent on teaching kids first and foremost good manners and respect. Should he dislike someone, whether justified or not, he won't go out of his way to talk to them. If he is neither here or there with someone, he still probably won't talk to them, but if he likes someone, then he is on their side and they won't be rid of him. I have to say, in many cases, his inclinations towards certain people are sound.

Some have said that to have Malc on your side is to gain two points a game. People seem much inclined to want to please him, such is the respect he commands; I have heard similar said about Brian Clough, and the comparisons are palpable. I often tease him, telling him how, like Clough, he is an eccentric fool. He pretends to hate this accusation but I know he secretly loves it.

To the people close to him though he is witty and bright, and in some respects the picture I have painted in this chapter is not a fair reflection of him. He admits that he has made mistakes, as anyone has, but hopes he may have learned from them. I for one have been given tremendous support by him over the years. He has encouraged, yet never pushed, and always supported me. We get on well now because of this. It makes achievements in New York even sweeter. It's a wonderful way to thank him for his efforts.

7 February 2010

Play Nick Matthew today in the Swedish Open Final. The billing has received more attention than usual as a reaction to our British Open Final in Manchester last year. The last 16 match in Saudi in December was our first meeting since, and as was alluded to in the pre-match introduction, many of the players turned up to watch; whether that was because they thought there was a decent chance of a fight, or whether it was because they assumed they might see a quality game would have been a subject of conjecture, but in any case it created interest. I have seen press releases of late which anticipate the British National Championships next week, highlighting the fact that our rivalry is ferocious and that the British Open was contentious.

If people sit up and listen because of the controversy then perhaps it can only be good for the game. Not every player gets along with every other and the press in squash circles, as good as they are, have tried in the past to hide any differences players harbour in order to preserve a clean image. Very little in modern life has a clean image nowadays, and certainly not if it wants to get noticed. Nothing and no one is perfect and exempt from the proverbial gutter, and the last thing the press at large want to put in their papers is how nice everyone is.

Publicity more often than not grows from seeds of controversy and negativity. Unfortunately if celebrity couples are happy and enjoying life, they will stand to receive less attention. Should such couples be in the midst of a divorce settlement, and at loggerheads, then ears will bleed as the story repeats itself incessantly in the many worldwide publications that are shoved in to our faces.

'People are never more interested in you than when you are up against the wall.'

The British Open final wasn't a high point. Losing was awful, like it always is, but I made it clear I was unhappy with Nick that night, and so at the time much was made of it. Nick and I have always been different animals and this manifests itself no more than on the court. His attitude that evening was unacceptable to me and I have never been the type of player to go for the 'what goes on court stays on court' theme.

The line of thought where players do and say what they like on court, only to be normal and friendly off it afterwards, is something to which I can't subscribe. There has to be one standard, one which is fair and respectful, but which doesn't compromise a player's aggression and competitiveness. People don't need to swear and shout at each other and start blocking and cheating in order to show passion.

It doesn't mean sacrificing toughness or manliness. It doesn't mean not contesting a decision with a referee. It doesn't mean not taking space on a shot when there is an open court (different to blocking). It doesn't mean being bland and dispassionate, and it doesn't mean not questioning an opponent's pick-ups. All of this is very much part of each individual player's personality; as long as a certain level of respect is retained, each player can give off their own signals in any way they please.

If a player is insistent on being pretentious and vicious on court, then I would rather keep to those same principles off it.

People have accused me of being too far on the other extreme, and some have frequently called me too nice. Perhaps they are trying to say that nice people don't get anywhere in life.

Whether it is a good or bad thing, in the immediate aftermath it doesn't feel natural to me to respond as if everything is normal off the court with a person who has treated me with disdain and arrogance on it.

I'm afraid it makes it worse still when a player shows disrespect to his opponent in a big match only to speak highly of them in press interviews and speeches afterwards. This amounts to insincerity. If players want to act so belligerently then so be it, but let's keep a distance from each other and not pretend afterwards.

A similar but less disconcerting incident played out with Frenchman Gregory Gaultier a few years back at the US Open, when I had beaten him in an acrimonious match where he accused me of blocking. For a time after I didn't want anything to do with him and he wondered why. As with Nick, and to be fair we have had few problems since, as time passes relations repair because we spend every other week with each other.

There was nothing that the audience would have deemed abhorrent in Manchester. There were no head butts in the warm-up or anything like that; it was more to do with the comments during the most contentious stages which bothered me. I'm not a sledger and I think it's fairly low, but I would rather be sledged at constantly throughout the match, rather than at specific stages. I can set my watch by certain players and their rants, and they creep in when I gain the ascendancy or retain parity.

Nevertheless, like it or not, my annoyance came over in the press interviews, and why shouldn't it? It's how I felt about the match. I glanced over the coverage the following day and found nothing of the comments anywhere. I discovered later that they thought it had been a heat of the moment thing and they didn't want to print words that later I might regret.

The press seem to be intent on preserving a clean cut

image, when it really doesn't do us much good. After concentrating on projecting a clean image for so long, we are further away from getting Olympic recognition than ever and the media are barely interested, so this seemed the perfect opportunity to run with it: two rivals from the same county whose relationship is now caustic. It appeared to be a solid chance to court controversy and attention.

Football, the highest profile game of all, is governed by bad behaviour, fall-outs and corruption. There is certainly no outward intention for the ugly game to retain any sort of clean image, yet does it do the sport any harm?

Rod Gilmour, writing for *The Telegraph*, did publish what I said in the interview alongside Nick's comments. My dad also had his say of course, and he piled in to Nick in his article for SquashSite. I couldn't help but agree with him on this occasion.

I went to Cairo the following Friday in pieces, mentally and physically. My body was achy and crooked, my feet blistered, and I had no inclination to play squash. I was desperately disappointed to lose another British Open having had match balls.

The trip will not go down on my list of highlights as a squash player. I had no will to practice or exercise, and even less to communicate.

Perhaps I should say a word about the squash in that British Open final, though, which was excellent. It was the first all-English final for 70 years, in a tournament previously seen as the de facto world championships before the World Open first surfaced in the late Seventies. It was a sell-out and the atmosphere was electric. We played for two hours and two minutes, well over the average time for a PSA world tour match (it is worth also noting that the men and women's tours now play point-a-rally to 11). By the end of it I had lost my second British Open final in succession. I was so, so close but eventually succumbed 8-11, 11-8, 7-11, 11-3, 12-10.

Nick said he didn't play well, I thought I played out of my skin. It was desperately tough, two players not ready to give an inch. I have enormous respect for Nick's squash and his dedication to what he does. The match itself was brutal; I didn't recover for weeks, and if it had all been about that it would have been a monumental occasion for both of us. Unfortunately it was memorable for the wrong reasons.

In Cairo it appeared that word had got around; people asked how I was, and they asked what all the problems were about. I had calls from my brother David, and as part of the England national coaching team he asked how we could resolve this problem before the World Team Championships, due to start in a matter of days.

'I don't know. I'll get on with it, and so will he. We aren't going to be walking around holding hands.' I didn't know what else to say. 'We play as individuals, and we'll be fine. I won't sit in a corner on my own; I'll join in with the team when appropriate, and as much as I usually do.'

On my return from Cairo I took a call from David Pearson, national coach, who was trying to build bridges in time for the event. The funding that squash receives is very much influenced by performances at the world teams and so he was keen to rectify the problems. I told him my thoughts. He asked me what the next step was. Should we fix a meeting? I said no, and that we would both be professional and civil in Denmark. A few days later Nick called me. It was a staggered conversation, and neither of us wanted to give much. He certainly wasn't going to say he was out of line, but rather his aim was to settle things before the event. It felt as if it had been encouraged by the coaches.

We bumbled through the world teams, but Nick got badly injured, dealing a major blow to our hopes. Of course, because we came fourth it was crisis time from every angle, everyone thinking we had no team spirit and that we were lacklustre and didn't get behind each other. Alister Walker and Adrian Grant were also on frosty terms at that point, which added fuel to the fire. All in all the World Teams was a disaster. We finished fourth and the quicker we could get home the better.

TWO

THOSE TRUSTY HANDS

8 February 2010

I had to retire injured against Nick, at 2-0 down. Conceding the final of one of Europe's biggest events, one that is brilliantly organised, massively supported and transmitted live on Swedish TV, is not funny. I know it is not my fault, but I feel that I have let people down. I slept for one hour.

Back in Leeds early, I have been booked in with Alison Rose, my trusty injury-busting physio, and the race to be fit for the British National Championships is on. She has a day and a half.

I first met Ali at the English Institute of Sport (EIS) in Sheffield in 2003. Strong-minded and confident in her knowledge, she was at the time working as a multi-sport physio there, and I aligned myself with her immediately. I have seen many physios during my career; some good, some excellent and some useless.

I immediately took to Alison's 'hands on' methods. It was clear that her commitment and conviction carried through to each of her patients. Unlike many physios that I had come into contact with during my time, short cuts were out of the question. Some physios would make it their prerogative to see as many patients as possible within the hour, offering a diluted service. Some, when they had run out of ideas, would panic and wire patients up to an ultrasound machine hoping for results. Alison has never given me anything but her full attention.

Alison often administers painful massage to her patients, and I can attest to having been in considerable pain during her sessions, to the point where I've drawn blood on my arm from biting it so hard. I have often exclaimed that I can see a dark smile on her face in reaction to my agitated vociferations, as she relentlessly ploughs her elbow into my hip.

Early on I found that my body responded to Alison's work and we soon had a routine. We were in the business of injury prevention rather than cure, and I was soon seeing her every week when at home. Even at a relatively young age, I was knowledgeable with regard to caring for the body, and how much treatment and attention I would need to give it.

I had worked with Damon Leedale Brown since I was 16 (he was then head strength and conditioning coach for England Squash), and his knowledge of the science of training for squash had been drip-fed to me over the years. If I do continue to lead a healthy life playing this sport for much longer, then Damon and Alison, and latterly Mark Campbell, together with EIS and England Squash and Racketball physios Jade Elias and Phil Newton, are the people to whom I would owe the greatest debt. The accumulation of time spent with these five people – conversing, receiving treatments from, and asking questions of them – would be impossible to quantify. Their impact on my squash career has been immense.

I realised as a young man that if I were to succeed, being so big – at 6' 4'' I am the tallest on tour – and heavy and with the body shape I had been given, then the training would need to be specific, smart and tough. I also figured that reaching and maintaining fitness at world-class levels would be no easy feat with my physical constitution, as dictated by Mother Nature.

Alison may sound quite barbarous, but there is far more to her than brute force. She constantly endeavours to move on in her field; she has a scrupulous tendency to learn and not get left behind, regularly giving up paid work and, at considerable expense to herself, doing some course or other at the opposite end of the country. The word stagnant could never apply. She regularly takes on new techniques and ideas and if ever she feels that someone is better able to help a patient, she will say so. This mindset is highly unusual in any coach, physio or player – protected egos are common in sport – but she is happy to delegate where necessary.

In fact this trait is absolutely necessary within any successful operation. Consider Clive Woodward's England rugby team of 2003, who diligently grafted and researched their way to World Cup victory. Woodward had every base covered during that tournament, prudently thinking that he was ill-equipped to lead every detail himself. He even flew over a team chef. How I would love that!

Squash is entirely different, and it isn't financially viable to be taking chefs everywhere, but I endlessly endeavour to utilise advice from many solid sources, and have gathered a team of people who offer different influences around me. There are six or seven who are always there for me, who are experts in their fields, and because of this support I give myself a solid chance of becoming the best. At the EIS in Sheffield one of many quotes on the walls reads: 'It's amazing just what can be achieved when nobody cares who takes the glory'.

As a child Malc ran everything to do with my squash. I was coached by him and guided by him, but in a healthy way. He realised that hitting the squash ball was his area of expertise, but he knew that up to date training methods, or nutrition perhaps weren't. He steadily relinquished his role as I grew older, not easy for any coach at first, and why should it be when they nurture and are successful with a player, only to see university graduates in the form of sports scientists and psychologists, with far less background in squash, come along and share the limelight?

I can see why coaches might feel threatened and cynical, and I have done myself, but the least you can do is listen.

Malc, as I did, learned for himself, and he saw that other coaches, other people, could help in different ways. I have always worked with my brother David, whose training is juxtaposed perfectly against Malcolm's work with me. It is reckless for any sportsman or woman to close themselves off to everything and to feel they know all they need to. It is quite staggering how much I have learnt and continue to learn about making myself the best possible player.

Alison asks me about my problems.

'What have you been doing now?' she said, half bantering.

'Where do you want me to start? First game in yesterday's final I lunged heavily for a low ball, and my rib muscle stung and really hurt. That seemed to subside and then I cramped in my shoulder. I took some massage at the interval and then that was OK. In the second game my inner thigh started to seize. Basically, "complete breakdown" are the words which spring to mind.'

She did all her tests on me, while I remained taciturn. All the while I'm hoping the situation is retrievable. I love the British Nationals, it's a big event and I'd be devastated not to make it.

Alison worked with me for two hours that day, and in the meantime I applied my focus to the rehab exercises, on mats, bored through my teeth but also hopeful of their impact. I ploughed through the exercises over and over, firing up the weakened muscles. 'Little and often', she had said. I even got into bed in the evening, and then told Vanessa I needed to do some more, at which she laughed. I didn't care how silly this was, though; if it would enable me to walk on to the court at the weekend in Manchester I would do the exercises all night long.

Alison had thought a pilates session would do me no

harm, and since they were running one at the clinic I gladly took part. She was happy with the progress we had made in little more than 24 hours. I had been out of sync yesterday; bones were tilted in my upper body, causing much stress lower down, explaining why the adductor faltered, all no doubt related to the volume of matchplay and travel of late.

Injuries are an athlete's worst nightmare. I will go to any lengths not to get injured, often manically concentrating on stability and core work (rehab exercises) far more incessantly than is normally required, but if it allows me to enter the squash court fit and healthy I will do what the situation prescribes. A period of injury is so entirely depressing that it makes losing feel like a night out with best friends.

People take the piss out of me for the amount of work I do off court – my warm-ups can be longer than my matches – because my paranoia does stretch to outlandish extremes at times, but I won't be worrying about that. In this age of information, there is much an athlete can do to avoid injuries, within his or her training structure, and through the funding programme in England we have spent time learning about this side of the game.

I clearly remember my England compatriot Peter Barker being asked in an interview if he thought he had been fortunate to have, up until that time, escaped serious injuries; his sagacious response was: 'No, I don't think I have been necessarily lucky. The type of training I have done has allowed me, to some extent, to not get injured'. He was right: his training had been smart, and therefore his reward was a sound body. Of course, some injuries can't be avoided however hard an athlete works and, unhappily, injuries manifest themselves through sheer bad luck. The good thing is that, being born in to an age of relative knowledge (compared to say the 1970s) gives today's athlete advantages, from which they can do all in their power to maintain a fit, healthy and injury-free body.

In time, no doubt, we will learn even more, to the point where the knowledge we have today will seem archaic. Soon there will be iPods that do the physiotherapy for you.

13 February 2010

Over the last three days I have been concerning myself with rehab, the very dull phenomenon where one sits about in gyms and on mats doing strange exercises repeatedly in an attempt to quash the effects of an injury, and receiving treatment from Jade, our EIS physio on-site in Manchester. How I need her help now; the work she puts in for the England squash team is unfaltering. After the matches I have been enduring painful massages from Sylvan Richardson, a good friend and excellent massage therapist who works with Olympic cyclist Chris Hoy and Liverpool FC. He is the musical director of the pop band I play in, Lost For Words and a former guitarist for Simply Red.

I played Daryl Selby, my in-form England team-mate, and controlled the match fluently and accurately to win 3-1 after a tough first game. So the work has been done, and I have neatly avoided any recurrence of recent issues through my diligence off the court this week. I can do little else now but play in the final tomorrow against Nick yet again, but all I think about is the dire horror of last Sunday when I conceded in Sweden, which sends waves of self doubt and unrest within the walls of my gut. What if it happens again? People travel from miles around to watch this event and if I fall prematurely through injury (again) just think of the disappointment I will cause.

In fact these thoughts penetrate my mind so wildly that I

have to stop myself by sweeping them out, replacing them with positive phrases aloud to counteract the negativity.

'It will be fine, your body is strong, Alison and Jade are convinced nothing is wrong. Think of all the work you have given your body, which will today enable you to stay strong and not break down. And if something does go wrong, then it is not your fault; you have done everything in your power to be fit.'

I am talking to myself again. In the words of Freddie Mercury: 'I'm going slightly mad.'

So I am consumed more by whether my body will maintain itself through a ravaging physical onslaught from Nick than the result or the squash, and I am drained by it. Just to be able to play is the only important thing and I haven't given the slightest thought to anything tactical; the times back in September where the body and mind were fresh after a summer of training, unclogged by endless bouts of matches, when I lived, ate and breathed the game, are over for now. Any time off court is either spent rehabbing or forgetting completely about squash.

What if all those people turn up and I can't get through the match? If only they knew, preparing now to come for their day out at the squash, they might not bother to make the journey.

The positive chantings make me feel better, though. Like a little child who wants the light on, or asks for his teddy bear at night, I need comfort, confirmation. I suspect all the players need their comfort blanket. We present a hard exterior to each other; our big tough, testosterone ravaged constitutions often dictate it to be so, but we need our teddies, just like anyone else.

14 February 2010

At Sportcity, walking towards the centre, I saw people arriving to watch and an avalanche of negative thoughts rained in on me. I thought about these people: 'you might be going home sooner than you think, if my body doesn't do as its told', and by flipping the thought round and adding an undertone of humour, the negative was reversed, again quickly lending me a sense of hope.

Disturbing thoughts dominated my faltering mind when I saw an excited young boy and his dad, unknown to me, and pondered how the father might have bought his son the tickets for a surprise, perhaps a birthday present: a ticket to the National Championships final in Manchester. Unbeknown to them one of the finalists is in pieces, mentally if not physically. The boy could have been looking forward to this, not sleeping because of the excitement, just as I did as a child.

Again I swept the thought out, and replaced it with those of a more positive kind, discovering a jolt of perspective.

It is only a game and you are healthy so just do your best.

I thought of Pontefract members who were so supportive and then I thought of Bev, my friend who is suffering from ovarian cancer, the same form of cancer my mother Lesley died of 10 years ago. Bev steadfastly endures more chemo as I write, and I think of her worries, and my own just pale in comparison.

I watched three games of the women's final between Jenny Duncalf and Alison Waters. The match oozed quality, was fiercely contested and entertaining. The two English girls displayed tenacious combat on the glass court in front of an eager crowd, providing a thrilling finish, which Alison won.

Would I be able to do the same? Or, as in Sweden last week, will I disappoint again?

At 4:10pm I began taping my ailing leg before registering an urge to tape my feet, hoping to prevent blisters. Why tape my feet? I don't need to and I haven't all week, so why now? What is my mind doing? I can always depend on myself for a laugh.

I made my drinks, and we strode onto court into a typically electric Manchester atmosphere. Come on, there are people who have more than a dodgy thigh to worry about.

I played the match as hard as I could but was found out in three games: 11-5, 11-6, 11-6. I didn't have the physical capabilities that I needed to compete with him.

'He is one of the best specimens in the sport. He's a tremendous athlete,' I offered afterwards.

I felt that I could have done little else to affect the outcome, and said as much to the reporters. It was disappointing that the match didn't live up to the atmosphere, or people's expectations of what they seem to enjoy christening 'a Valentine's Day rivalry' between the two of us, a rivalry that is starting to feel rather one-sided. But I could not be upset with what I had done all week. He was indomitable. I was flat.

I hit a low after the loss, and the feeling of anti-climax at the end of the event, the nothingness in the venue after the buzz of the week's play compounded the dejection. Luckily for squash players there is always another tournament around the corner to which to look forward. Athletes and boxers, naming two examples, who compete with much less regularity than squash players, must be beside themselves after a major competition, with so little to look towards in the near future.

I enjoyed the night, taking the chance to relax with my pal Nathan, at Ponte. There were a few of the members drinking at the bar who had come to the match and I felt their disappointment. They felt mine, gave me their opinions which can be grossly off the mark at times, but as Mick tells me, they want the best. I find it difficult not to respond to these opinions that they always seem so inclined to give. I wonder why they think they have any idea of how difficult it is to maintain a world class standard in anything.

17 February 2010

I wake up and instantly the brain begins to process that today is to be my first day of training for quite some time, since 16 January I think. The last month, densely packed with competitive play and travel, has left my legs feeling as if they could do with some work. After a couple of days off, I waddle out of my warm bed, glance outside to see drab Leeds skies, knowing this is likely to be a tough one. After no training for such a time, today is a novelty. During runs of competition, training is more sparse and merely topped up here and there. Apart from the tough matches, tournaments are actually a welcome break from the daily back to back training efforts of the off season.

My bones creak as I walk downstairs. The stairs of our house are too small for my big feet to fit, so I descend carefully sideways, bobbing my head under the doorway at the bottom. I take a big bowl of mixed cereals for breakfast, pack my bags and I'm in the car at 8:45am.

This morning I'll be working with Mark Campbell, the Kiwi lead strength and conditioning coach at the English Institute of Sport in Sheffield, who is so sadistic that he likes to instil pain to professional athletes on a daily basis. It is his living. He is assuredly brilliant at what he does and has my total confidence.

I've been working with Mark for a year and a half and he has been instrumental in guiding the recovery process after last year's injury. Not only are his workouts varied and interesting, they are integral in maintaining fitness and strength throughout long seasons of squash. By producing strong athletes, Mark ensures that they are equipped to handle heavy work loads. I remember him saying that if any of his athletes pick up injuries, a thigh strain for example, he questions himself because he knows such injuries can be avoided through smart training.

I enjoy his training immensely, despite his propensity to include chin-ups in my programme. Weighing 90 kilos, as I do, does not lend itself to doing chin ups! I can clearly see by the look on his face the exact moment he is to administer a set of chin ups and I search for excuses. Like Alison, he takes fiendish satisfaction from the pain he inflicts and I tell him in the nicest possible way that he is a bastard.

In many respects Mark is uncomplicated with regard to his training methods, but each session is approached with great thought and application, and every single exercise is designed to maximise the athlete's performance in their sport. His most subtle and skilful faculty is the ability to mix sessions so that they are always different, retaining the interest and focus of the athlete whilst also stressing the body in different ways. Repeating the same session constantly is dull, and the older I get the more variation I need.

With only a couple of days before I travel to Richmond, Virginia, on Friday, Mark commissions a mixed session of squats and lunges with weights, which are kept light so soon before an event. And, in view of the prospect of a tough session with David this afternoon, I do core and stability exercises with rotation, medicine ball throws and mini-circuits to finish, giving the lungs a minor blow out.

Training is a complex subject on which I am regularly questioned, mostly by amateur players searching for quick answers. Such things do not exist, of course. Science has hugely improved the training we do for sport; indeed to cover all I have learnt on that subject over the years would warrant the writing of a separate book completely.

Training for professional squash players now is vastly different to what it was 10, 20, and 30 years ago. In the Seventies and Eighties, players were famous for doing exhausting sessions involving endless repetitions of 400m sprints, or hour and a half long court sprint sessions. Jansher and Jahangir Khan, the two greatest Pakistani squash players, talked about running for five miles, playing ten games of squash, running back home, before playing matches in the afternoons. This sort of regime is torturous and would be considered detrimental today. I have a feeling they might well have been exaggerating when revealing their training regimes, but their work rate was undoubtedly monstrous. To declare that they put themselves through such daily rigours probably put the fear of God in opponents before they had even stepped on court.

Jonah Barrington, one of the greats of the game in the Seventies, was said to have run three miles just before a match and I have heard him say that he would doubt if any squash player has trained any harder than he did. Geoff Hunt, Jonah's legendary Australian contemporary, was rumoured to be running 40 sets of 400m sprints in one session. Ouch. Small wonder that Geoff and Jonah have both had serious hip problems and fought with injuries ever since, battle scars visible from the way they walk today. Jonah and Geoff may claim to have trained just as relentlessly as any other athlete in the history of sport, but these methods weren't the smartest or the safest, and by punishing themselves daily with this frightening regime, longevity was always going to be a problem.

Of course, Geoff and Jonah were incredible physical athletes, among the greatest ever, and I don't say that lightly. Even though their mental and physical capacity was outrageous, there was surely little emphasis on specific movement training, functional strength work or core stability, if only for the reason that nobody knew what these things were, but all of which nowadays are part of any serious athlete's training regime.

This side of training is probably the most important aspect of my programme. Of course, the routines, match practice, and specific brutal feeding sessions (where the coach hits balls for me to retrieve) are vital; in the end playing squash is what we do, but I would have been far worse off without the knowledge of this off court work, the constant repetition of which keeps my body strong, flexible and healthy. I feel lucky to have had this knowledge. Geoff and Jonah had to work everything out for themselves, and because squash is so hard, they naturally figured that working themselves to death was the best thing to do.

A strength workout now consists of lunges with rotations, medicine ball throws and strength through the core; any session revolves largely around squats and split squats with heavier weights which teach the body to increase power output, allowing me to be explosive onto the ball. A session will include squash specific plyometric exercises (high impact, high speed movements) so that I can transfer that power to the court.

Lunges are the main exercise, with or without weights, as it is being the most common movement in squash. However, it makes sense to train this movement in a controlled way. All these exercises encourage the primary muscles used in a game of squash to stay strong throughout the course of a match. I focus on the glutes (backside muscles which often get weak) and core muscles (around the stomach), calves, ankles and shoulders, which absorb a lot of work through the hitting of the ball.

The science of training for squash, of which so much has been learned in the last few years, makes total sense. Years and years of playing a brutal game in which twisting, turning, heavy lunging, stressing the poor joints in a way that humans were probably not designed to, invites weaknesses, imbalances and stresses to take hold of the body. And if the body does not have the strength to withstand the pressure, problems inevitably follow. All this functional, sensible training helps to keep me balanced and strong so that maximum strength, power and endurance is maintained in a match, and the chances of staying injury free for longer are higher.

And I warm-up of course. If club players warmed-up in a specific and functional way consistently before matches, I would go as far as to say it would add five years to their sporting lives, and give them fewer back problems to boot. Warm-ups are grossly underrated, and many people are convinced that they are too busy to do them, which is rubbish. As a squash player, a correct warm-up is the single most important thing anyone can do for the health of their body.

I learnt an important lesson from Jonah on the importance of warming up as a young boy. Aged 16, I went up to Aberdeen with a friend to watch the British Open, where apart from being entranced and absorbed by watching the top players, I spent time with Jonah.

He and my dad have been friends for many years, and we had spent time at each other's houses in the past, so I knew him well. He took me on court for a session at the local sports centre, and it has remained a quite unforgettable experience. The one thing that occupies my most vivid recollection of that day was Jonah's warm-up: the gusto and dedication with which he, nearly sixty at the time, applied himself to just that part of the session, was astonishing. It left quite an imprint on my young mind. His warm-up, consisting of ghosting sets and stretching, nearly overlapped the allotted time that I had deemed would be normal for the whole session. In that couple of hours with Jonah, hanging with bated breath on his every move and word, I could hardly have been offered a more pertinent message as to the level of dedication and application required to be really good, or like him, great.

Through his actions he taught me a most valuable lesson: if one wants to be great, incredibly good, or even plain good, then commitment, practice, constant repetition and hard work simply cannot be avoided. The great genius sportsmen and women in history all have one thing in common and what's more they all admit as much: that talent can only be nothing without hard work. No great sportsman, not ever, not anywhere, has succeeded on talent alone.

I'm one half of the day down. I am driving to Halifax in the afternoon, post-lunch and the next session is due to be a tough one with David. I do different types of sessions with him: sometimes they are group based with other players, sometimes they are more technical and less physical, where we may hit balls and discuss things to work on, analyzing finer points of the game. Other times, like today, they are more physical.

I have learnt a lot about the subtleties of the sport during our more technical sessions in which we have worked on areas to enlarge my game through using deception, holding of the ball before the shot and increased racket head speed. It is important at the highest levels not to become one dimensional, and today's current top ten all have different facets on which to rely. Simply having one way of playing won't cut it.

Nevertheless, today is a physical day. I try to listen to the radio but all I can think of is this bloody session. This particular drive always brings about a sick feeling in my stomach because of the physical hurt the session is likely to bring about.

Halifax, like Pontefract, is one of those towns I find it possible to love and hate all at once – my outlook on hard training is much the same – a town which somehow suits the slate grey skies that more often than not shroud the place. Halifax doesn't look quite right in sunshine, a reality to which Yorkshire folk have become quite accustomed. Yorkshire people now identify so strongly with their environment – a mix of industrial towns and generally indecisive weather – that they are almost affectionate and nostalgic towards it.

I drive, and I see the same signs, the same shop windows, the same pubs that I always see, all of which I associate with pain and unhappiness. Stopping at a red light, I look into the shops and often wonder if changing jobs would be at all plausible; a desk clerk, perhaps, just for one afternoon, sipping coffee at will. Biscuits.

But I can't. I know there is only one option and that is to go through with the pain. That is sometimes the frightening thing. I know I am mentally strong enough to go through with it. Otherwise it signals failure, or at least that's how I view it. But I know only too well the rewards that may come my way on the other side, and therefore I absolutely need it and love it. An 'investment', some like to call it.

'Every shot back to me. I'll feed from the back right,' David declares. In many respects, this is the worst part of the session, the beginning. It is the part at which there is the longest possible time to go, and it is worse when the body isn't fully warm. I find it hard to move quickly early on. A shock to the system. Still in the car.

David pushes his feeding quicker, and I have to go with it. To some extent the player, however hard the coach makes it, can control the pace. If I don't make a concerted effort to push myself, he can't always do it for me. Soon I get into it though and we both start to hit a good pace. We are pushing out forty five seconds or one minute sets, him feeding boasts, drives, drops, all inch-perfect in their placement in the corners, and me hitting back to his quarter.

'We are taking the rests down. You will only get 15 to 20 seconds, if that. We need this to be as realistic as possible. That's all you ever get in between rallies.'

Christ, I think. I don't talk because I can't.

We repeat and repeat the sets, and with only four down, my legs show signs of tying up. It continues to baffle me that, despite all my training over the years, this sport can still render me exhausted within ten minutes. I suppose that's part of the lure of the game. Not many sports can do that to anyone.

My only motivation is the couple of minutes' rest David gives me every now and then. I look forward to that simple period of time. When it happens I breathe loudly and heavily, sipping water and towelling down off court. What excuse can I use to prolong the rest? Some water, I'll get some water.

We are back on doing a different feeding set. I lunge about, dragging my body around. I hit everything straight. David feeds the ball into the front half and mid court, at serious pace now. I start to dislike him. In between sets I swear. I start to find I quite like the short rests rather better than the long ones in a funny way, as the less time I have the less I think about the dire fatigue that engulfs me.

I try to concentrate on the quality of my squash in this situation. It is easy to get wrapped up in the physical aspects of the session. It is not meant to be merely a beasting. I try to focus on quality rather than quantity.

It is pure pain now. The ball, as much as I try to keep it accurate, is going all over the place. I focus on keeping steady in my shots, to try to get the balls up and in good places, despite the paralysing tiredness that besets me. After all it is no good getting there if I can't hit accurately at the end of it. This is what is so good about these feeding sessions: they encapsulate what needs to be done on the court and are as specific as it gets.

After the second rest I start to perk up, going through my strongest period. The finish line is not as far away now. Every minute I am a step closer to lying prostrate on the floor, recovering, session over.

The fourth block is severe but I push as hard as I can. After every set I keel over, hands on knees, willing oxygen into my lungs. I think about tomorrow being a rest day, and how heavenly that will be. I know there is a final flourish at the end of this session. I keep pushing.

'Shot and a ghost to finish James. Six sets of eight.'

I ghost, (running in to a lunge without the ball, mirroring the shot) to one corner and then he feeds me a shot to another, this time with the ball. He gives me such little rest in between each set that I cannot recover. This exercise is more in straight lines. I know where I am going to be moving, but physically it is the most punishing of the lot. It's classic, savage squash training.

We complete the sets and I am at death's door with pain. He shakes my hand. 'Well done Jimbo. It's in the bank.' I get Jimbo now and not James. I cannot get off the court quick enough. We sit down, David smiles wryly and I know what's coming. 'Finish off on the stepper?'

Without even the slightest protest, as I know it will be of no use and will only serve to tire me further, I trudge over to the gym, and finish myself completely with sets on the stepper machine. Whoever invented the thing needs bloody shooting. A stepper day means that tomorrow will be a washout. As I finish on the stepper, in a dire state, what the session demands is almost beyond me. At the moments of the most extreme pain I think of giving up but know I can't. The body has a remarkable way of adapting to training and it is surprising what the body can get through when the mind lets it.

Conversely, the trip back is almost one of great elation; a freedom that I can drive home, happy in the knowledge that there is a hard session in the bank. Halifax becomes a beacon. The sun might even shine, and the signs and sights I now view positively. I can go home, see Vanessa, relax, and enjoy a good hearty meal. Even a few chores perhaps. I'm ready for anything, in a good frame of mind, despite being absolutely physically exhausted.

It is often said that the feeling of exercise promotes or releases endorphins which make a person feel good, and can often solve the greatest depression. I absolutely endorse this. People who do have tendencies to feel down can do worse than spend an hour exercising.

David has been a major motivator to me during my career, and I can't thank him enough for the afternoons he has diligently spent with me sowing the seeds. I very much hope that one day his years of dedication will yield a world No 1 and a world champion out of me.

19 February 2010

Again I am lumbered with time and baggage at Manchester airport, as I prepare for the flight to Richmond, Virginia. After all these years I still seem incapable of packing light, so I brace myself for yet another excess baggage fee. The reason I give is the fact that my size 13 shoes take up so much room. I end up paying the fee; no one seems to accept this as discriminatory, but people with smaller feet have no such issue, or can at least pack more shoes.

The plane ride is a bloody nightmare. Every person on the plane seems to be coughing or sniffling. I change seats at least three times, only to find that someone near the seat I move to is also sneezing. I have always been susceptible to infections, as many athletes are, so when I am nearing a tournament, in fact most of the time, I become so preoccupied with not catching a cold that it becomes slightly obsessive. I even walked out of a restaurant just before one World Open because the waiter was so full of cold: eyes all popping out of his head and bloodshot. I was livid – what the hell he was doing coming to work and serving food in such a state I had no idea. It was ghastly. I left Vanessa there to eat her sandwich on her own, while I sulked in the car.

A word about my obsessive tendencies when it comes to illnesses: I have a frustrating habit of contracting chest infections and this has been the case since my infancy. A couple of years ago I consulted the EIS doctors and nutritionists to see if there was anything I could do to prevent the onset of the infections, and as a result I have a list of supplements and rituals as long as my arm to ward off the nasty bugs. Infections amongst athletes are not uncommon as they are particularly susceptible, mainly because of the high volume of training, which continuously depletes the immune system. The doctors assured me that full time athletes can contract four or five upper respiratory tract infections a year. I was relieved to hear it.

When, if ever, I finish playing squash, I will be thoroughly delighted with three things:

1. Food: not having to watch what I eat.
2. The elimination of brutal training sessions.
3. Not having to think about catching a cold, or getting injured.

My paranoia takes many strange forms: there is the compulsive need I have to repeatedly wash my hands, especially when travelling. I also carry sinus inhalers (legal ones) everywhere I go and take about four supplements a day. I often lose track of what I have and haven't taken, becoming confused and breaking out in sweats. In the end the process can become so wearisome that I have to laugh at myself.

25 February 2010

It's good to finally get playing in Virginia.

I beat Alister Walker convincingly 3-0, and the match was niggly. He was pushing his weight around a bit, and gave me a couple of knocks in the match, with little acknowledgement of the fact. There's no harm in asking a player if he is okay after a collision, accidental or not. Instead he decided to talk to the referee.

It's France's Gregory Gaultier in the quarters, who took me to the cleaners in Hong Kong in November; a 3-0 drubbing, and a convincing one at that. I was livid post match, snapping at Malcolm unnecessarily and taking it out on him. In turn he snapped at Gaultier if I remember rightly, when Greg had merely asked for the bus times; consequently Malc and I bickered our way through the Hollywood plaza shopping mall as we tried to find transport back to the hotel.

How glamorous that venue is – with crowds hanging over each floor to get a view of the glass court on the ground floor atrium below – but I wanted to be anywhere else after that loss. It really hurt and I didn't talk to anyone for hours, preferring to sulk. I was out of the country in a flash.

I had done some work on it though, and found my study paid off. Not many people manage to beat Greg 3-0, which I did tonight. Whether he is said to be out of form or not, I'm happy to take it.

27 February 2010

Had a day off after my semi-final defeat against Nick. I have rarely felt more uncomfortable against him and didn't have control at any stage. Frenzied and outfoxed, I was on the end of a dismantling, and was short of ideas. Just as I had administered a display to discomfort Greg the previous day, I was on the receiving end of a similarly emphatic defeat. The physical problems were less of an issue this time, possibly because I went in to this particular match fresh, but it is more worrying to be beaten by him on squash.

Tactically I was bereft, and he was anything but. I will surely and rapidly speak more to Malcolm on this and watch the match on video. I have nothing important to focus on so I revert to alcohol. I go for weeks on end striving with such intensity on all aspects of the game and this substance provides the extreme that I need at the end of it.

This curious chemical is my preferred sleep inducer at present. There are many functions at this tournament so I might as well take advantage of the free booze. I won't sleep if I don't, anyway, and I am not comfortable taking more sleeping pills.

For most of the night I stand apart, watching. This is something I have grown accustomed to and it is a situation with which I feel most comfortable. There is occasional conversation but on my part it is fairly pitiful. I converse amiably enough with one or two patrons and sponsors, but soon they find a reason to regress. Crowds of people who talk together seem to have a habit of closing up on shy, awkward giant types like me. I like being tall but my size makes the social ineptness more blatant. This sort of thing used to upset me back in the sensitive cherub days, but now, slightly more hard-nosed, I am entirely happy on my own, no longer fighting it, rather often bolting for the nearest dark corner on such social occasions. The drink helped, and David and I ended the night with a chat to Greg at the hotel, and it seemed he had also taken this opportunity to relax.

THREE

DEALING WITH HURT

3 March 2010

Mick has arranged for me to play an exhibition with the great Peter Nicol in Dublin on behalf of my racket sponsor Prince. I couldn't have been more pleased with how it went. It was a hard day, no doubt, but the kids we coached from 2:30 til 6 were a delight. They were interested, respectful and charming. The crowd enjoyed the match in the evening, or at least they appeared to, and the collective good feeling around the place over the day and a half was fantastic. I am thrilled that I made the effort to go over there, such was the response, and I hope it made a difference to the people involved.

4 March 2010

Visited Oscar Wilde's birth place. Having an extra day in Dublin, I couldn't resist getting a little closer to someone whose genius I have always admired.

6 March 2010

I trained at Pontefract and Malc took offence at some of my idiosyncrasies. For instance, the fact that I often ask to warm the ball up during a session after having had a break seems to upset him. From his reaction I can only surmise that he feels it is some kind of personal attack on his balls. It really isn't, simply the ball goes cold. For the rest of the session he continued to make comments intimating that in fact the ball looked 'lively', and I got pissed off. When I started to look particularly despondent he asked 'When you practise with David, are you this intense?'

'I've no idea', I replied. He thinks I am and I tell him that squash is that sort of game. He is all about relaxing all of the time. Rhythm. I like a mix. There has to be an element of intensity if it is to translate onto the squash court at the highest levels.

Later on, he said on a whim that he thought I didn't 'fit in' here now. He implied that the way I like to work is not conducive to the way things are done at Pontefract. I let it go. Sometimes I feel these tensions emanate from my gradual deviation from Pontefract. I don't get there as often, partly because I live in Leeds, partly because I am always in a different country and this probably frustrates him, though he is reluctant to say it, and he accedes that I have little alternative to leading such a life.

As I have become accustomed to this singular way of life, I don't doubt that I have changed quite markedly. I had to. Malc, in his sessions, doesn't like too much intensity: the boast drive practice is never done with either player moving to the T for example. I have probably become more severe, in many aspects, as the years have passed, which is why his sessions are good for me now.

His work retains so much value, but there are times when the intensity and concentration levels need to be through the roof. I agree with him that I may be too far the other way and so we could do with meeting halfway.

When two people work so hard and strive so diligently to achieve something special, wires inevitably get crossed and things get difficult. People might think things are worse in a father-son relationship, but in our case the difficult exchanges that we have are few. They will never be avoided altogether and how can they hope to be? Which

rock star, writer, artist or sportsman has ever succeeded
with everything being easy or perfect? I would say
none. There almost needs to be difficulties, tensions,
disagreements even, to propel the positive output of
anyone creative.

Malc's strengths lie in his understanding of professional
squash, his understanding of me as a person, and he is a
port of call for advice of any description. There have been
times where I have sulked my way through practice, or
where I have felt too low to play squash. Sometimes he has
taken me off the court for my misdemeanours, only to
bring me round with a thoughtful talk, trying to get to the
bottom of any trouble I feel.

His ability to know how much is too much, whether to
do with training or matchplay, is astute and very rare.
When I lose limply, or under-perform because I have done
too much, he is the first person to recognise it, and never
once has he not understood. That is very difficult for
anybody to grasp, let alone someone who can't claim to
have competed at the highest level; this proves that coaches
never need to have been a top player.

So, what's it like having your dad as a coach? This
question is often asked at exhibition nights that we have
done, and so I play up to it, and the crowd eat out of my
hand, feeling dreadfully sorry for me, as I make out that I
have been tortured all my life. 'How would you feel having
your dad, a controversial one-off, as a coach?'

As a young child there were standards of behaviour that
needed to and still need to be adhered to. As with all his
players, problems arose from the fact that I misbehaved;
there was never ever an issue about a result; winning was
of little interest to him, and he never cared how well I
played. As long as I conducted myself properly and tried
my best Malcolm would have no reason to reprimand me
in any way.

Unfortunately I was far from well behaved as a young sportsman. I was a little brat at times, but by the time I was 11 or 12 his persistent discipline had translated fully, to the point where I was much less of a problem. The dressing-downs and the bollockings (looking back every one was justified) encouraged the attitude I have on a squash court today, of calmness and few signs of emotion. I certainly thank him for instilling this attitude; it must have won me countless matches. There were many occasions in my younger years where I had to be taught severe lessons. Even at that time I showed signs of being complicated, difficult and sensitive.

My parents' separation made things difficult in my teenage years, and I suffered because he did. He probably didn't know it but I felt as if I was dealing with his pain and my own at the same time.

Our relationship, since my mother's death, has become stronger. We are now friends more than anything else, and apart from the odd problem our relationship works as well as it ever has. The reason it works, in a life where father-son professional relationships tend not to operate, is because I accept his knowledge of the sport and am always respectful of the admiration he commands.

Malcolm's working methods will not be implemented by many other coaches. There is no other coach the world over who works in the same way, except for his line of disciples.

The striking and obvious difference between Malcolm and other coaches is that he rarely coaches individually. His sessions are all done in groups, and they last for one to two hours, rather than 30 or 45 minutes. He is without question the most prolific manufacturer of young squash players in the world, and this group ethos is the reason. The sessions are cheaper, meaning kids can have more lessons in a single week; the kids enjoy them because they engage socially and have as much fun playing the sport as possible. Few ten year-old children want to be doing tiring and technically based one-to-one lessons repeatedly. They get more out of playing and interacting with their friends, and the hours the kids rack up through training with Malcolm in this way means they hit more balls and get better more quickly, without the process becoming dull.

At a professional level his sessions are the same. Saurav Ghosal, the Indian number one who trains at Pontefract, and I work with groups in the mornings when we are in the country. The mixed nature of these sessions creates new stimuli every day, and maintains a variation that sustains our enthusiasm for the sport. After training all my life, this helps counter any burnout effects.

Malc puts on a session every weekday morning at 10:30, meaning that if I land back in the country hardly knowing what day it is I know I don't have to start ringing round players and clubs for practice sessions. These sessions are there for his players all year round and this solid structure is a luxury that can be easily taken for granted.

There is a great difference in the standard of player that turns up at these sessions: they are often littered with big names, past and present, and at the same session might be a Leeds Metro Division 4 player. Malcolm does not judge everything by standard. He prefers that the people who come to his sessions are well mannered and behaved, with a level of aptitude that is a standard requirement rather than brilliant. He prides himself on mixing players together in his practice sessions. Occasionally he will put me on the court with a 12-year-old, who might feed me the ball. This might sound ridiculous to some, and I know many of the other professionals have laughed, but for me it is natural. When I was 12 I was lucky enough to practice with players of a far superior standard.

Malcolm will work us through until 12, and he will start again at 4pm with his juniors for an hour and a half, before going until 8pm with the adults. I tend to look after my own training in the afternoons, which may consist of match play, weights or strength and conditioning, or a session with David.

Technically speaking Malcolm has some quirks. He teaches and endorses rhythm and purity and encourages text book footwork: left foot lead on the right side, right foot lead on the left. He teaches a flat swing, often discouraging over-slicing the ball. The two of us don't always see eye to eye on these issues, but that's not the point. What matters is that we discuss it, rather than fall out over technicalities. It is a great testimony to him as a coach that he doesn't enforce strict rules, but instead nurtures players in the way that they are bound to be led. No two players of his are the same, and that shows his versatility.

Despite his technical leanings, he accepts that there are great players at the top of the world who do not go by his principles, and therefore his teachings are a guide.

21 March 2010
Canary Wharf Classic, London

Catch the train down to London. These days fill me with great excitement, and I genuinely feel fortunate to do what I do today. This week I will play matches in a beautiful glass court venue at Canary Wharf, staying in London for free, and I will earn money from it: all that remains for me to do is play my favourite sport. Some hardship.

The last three weeks' training have been hard, but now it feels worth it. To know that the work has been done provides me with a warm glow of confidence. There is little to do now but play.

I have to accept the fact that my body won't allow me to live this life forever, and I am aware that the clock ticks, obviating any onset of arrogance, or of taking such fortune for granted. I was 21 only yesterday, and now aged 27 I start to imagine the day when I might not be able to wake up in the morning and enjoy the excitement that comes with competing in big matches. Every day matters.

25 March 2010

London, specifically Canary Wharf, is my happy hunting ground. Once again I'm playing Nick in the semi-finals. I am on a losing streak of about 10 matches to him, but then so are most players. I have lost the last two matches convincingly, 3-0. There is some breathing space after this tournament so I can look ahead to relaxation.

'Get good starts. Have faith in what you can do', are the customary statements I hear from Malcolm as I warm myself up. Here we go again. What a circus this all is. Incredible tension mixed with excitement and anticipation are the primary feelings in the lead up to such a match.

As I get ready, a man approaches me, and politely implores me to 'beat Matthew this time'. I have never seen the man before, and while I appreciate the sentiment, I do not appreciate the timing. I wouldn't dream of interrupting a business meeting of theirs, and I'm sure no sports man or woman in any other professional sport accepts it. I'm not sure how people come to the conclusion that their words, those of a complete stranger, could be beneficial at such a stage. Squash players get a lot of this, I suppose because of our accessibility.

I lose the first 11-7, much in the same way that I often lose the first to him. Tough, tight, intense squash. I am not particularly disturbed, and neither is Malc, and it shows in the next game. I come out of the blocks fast and win the second convincingly, buoyed by the way the court is taking my shots with a slight deadness that I am enjoying. It's tough but I'm feeling fine. The quality of play is right up there. The third is a furious mental and physical battle. I take the lead 7-4 and then hold game balls at 10-7. In typical waspish fashion he gets back to parity and I know I am in a battle. What I don't know is that the game is barely half over. The tie-breaker turns the match into a monumental tussle – it includes one of the longest rallies on tour that year, too – and the loss of those leads will come back to hurt me later. Well into the second hour the balance tips both ways, back and forward. Nick saves seven game balls. I win the game 18-16, but at what cost? Its conclusion could have arrived sooner for me.

At 2-1 and 7-4 up in the third, I make an error which saps my energy. Again Nick claws his way back to take the game. Although I lose it, I do very little wrong, and his intensity rises a notch; his trademark grit comes to the fore. I am hanging on. I suspect he might be too. He has probably done a little more work than me. As I sit in my corner, Malc bellowing positive comments into my ear, urging me to be strong and tough, the pain and hurt hits me. The lungs, distressed, wage a fight against the very atmosphere for oxygen. The legs are getting heavier and feel leaden with deep fatigue. I down an energy shot gel, and as much water and sports drink as I can stomach. The body unfortunately does not push itself. Moving forward and getting onto balls early, for instance, is far harder now; I can just about do it, but the effort required to make it happen is so horribly hard to summon. Although adrenalin is somehow allowing my body to sustain the effort, my mind is struggling to believe I can go the distance.

This is the heat of the battle. I think to myself at one point that I don't feel quite as bad as I would have done at this stage 18 months ago, and feel pleased with my physical capabilities, which have improved through much hard graft.

Early in the fifth game I feel as if my left leg is about to cramp but it subsides just in time; 4-4 becomes 6-6, then 7-7 and I think for a moment that I should have picked up golf clubs or a snooker cue as a child, rather than a sodding squash racket. It may still be an option if I get practising.

I do not say this lightly, and I am generally quite critical if anything, but the match is of the very highest quality. I know inside that I have not played as well as this for some time, and realise that what we are both doing is special. At 8-9 down we have another monumental rally. Then all my fears unravel. I rotate around the middle of the court and lunge heavily into the back left trying to retrieve a deep ball from Nick. My left quad pulsates with an explosion of excruciating cramp. I writhe about the floor in agony.

Nick later tells me that after celebrating the winning rally, he thinks I may have broken something. His initial reaction from watching the replay sees him raise both arms to his face with that in mind. Cramp is not usually serious, but it is acutely painful for about 30 seconds. It is a way of the muscles saying that they have had enough. There are nutritional strategies that may help, but in a match that has been so unforgiving, with two players at the peak of their powers knocking seven bells out of each other, something eventually has to give. Nick, at 29, is older and physically more mature. But I am the one to fall first.

I realise after a couple of minutes of poking and prodding by the therapists, Caroline and Sylvan, with whom I have worked so much during my career, that I can't carry on. Nick has already sportingly offered me time to recover which I am not allowed, according to the rules. Malc tells me there's no way, while I writhe about. My quad is taking on an almost animalistic form, as the muscle appears, like an alien, to be bulging and trying to force its way out of my body. Sylvan is silently appalled at the contortions my muscle is making, and he feels that the quad is now redundant.

I shout at Malc to let me have a go at standing up, to give me a chance, and as soon as I do it is clear it is all over. I go to Nick to shake his hand and we half embrace, both fully aware of the standard we reached. Although we've had our differences this season, especially after the volatile British Open final, there was nothing wrong here. Nick did his stuff, berating the referee at intervals as he does, but in no way was it personal or offensive this time. It was just heavy squash, played in an aggressive way, but sportingly. So another two-hour battle. Another defeat, this time 11-7, 5-11, 18-20, 11-8 , 9-8 after 127 minutes – five minutes longer than our British Open tussle.

I was far from disappointed. There was no way I could be after a match like that. I train to win, of course I do, but I take great satisfaction in performing in that way, win or lose. It was one of my most accomplished performances, and not just this season. The British Open final was a quality match, but it wasn't in the same league as this one. In every player's career there may only be a handful of matches that are truly memorable, if they are lucky. People still talk to me animatedly about my English Open match with John White in 2004; others froth at the mouth when talking about my match with Ramy Ashour in the quarters of the Tournament of Champions in 2007. This one should slot nicely into this 'most talked about' category, if my judgment is anything to go by.

7 April 2010

I found myself absorbed in a programme about the holocaust last night, where one of the victims, a survivor of the camps, recounted a haunting story, painfully depicting acute malnourishment: during the death marches, they descended upon a place, hundreds of them together, in

desperate need of food. Frighteningly thin, their lives were
shaped by constant scrummaging for food. The man
recalled the moment that he found a pea, and telling no
one, he broke it in to four pieces, giving him a longer
'meal'. In three minutes the sensation of food in his mouth
had finished. As he described it, his expressions of that
'meal' were coloured with a euphoria, which at that time
translated to the viewer a feeling akin only to heaven.

As I sat watching I felt fat and greedy and contemplated the
thought of extreme hunger: a sensation many of us are terribly
lucky never to feel. I thought of putting myself through a fast,
as I indulged in my week off, sitting on the sofa.

9 April 2010

I am heading to Nice for two French League matches in
Marseille. A weekend of near solitude lies ahead.

Arriving in Nice I decide to drive to the city and have a
meal. The city landscape is dominated by a delectable
coastline and, having parked the car, and revelling in my
independence, I walk along the coastline as the sun sets,
unable to comprehend the inherent contrast between the
two cities that mark the beginning and end of my journey. I
am left in awe. The voices, the smells, the sunshine! Nice is
a definite holiday possibility. I wander up the coast, and in
to the old town.

The sun and the sky are mesmerising, people are outside
eating, drinking. I wander up and down thinking about
where to eat and after much examination and indecision
I decide on a restaurant, whittling it down by scrutinising
the menus, and considering which cater more for
vegetarians.

France is good for many things, but its unflinching
devouring of animals is repulsive. It is the only place I have

been interrogated by a waiter for wanting a baguette without ham.

They look at me as if I have asked to bring my pet dinosaur into the restaurant. I think about all the wondrous beauty and happiness that exists here in the social hub of Nice and my mind switches to thoughts of abattoirs, where animals are caged and mutilated.

In December 2007 I played for England in the World Team Championships in Chennai, India, a place where cows randomly roam the streets and the levels of hygiene are worlds apart. We would travel by car, observing donkeys trudging along with heavy carts and cows blocking the traffic, do our practice or play before returning to our four-star hotel to gorge on spaghetti bolognese for dinner. The most basic of questions suddenly became prominent in my mind: where did the meat that we happily devour every day come from?

It wasn't an altogether new question. For some time I had been thinking about food and its origins and had slowly developed an interest in nutrition. During the time of Mum's illness, she had started to buy organic produce to help herself, and I became more aware. By the time of the world teams in 2007 I avoided mass produced meats from supermarkets or restaurants.

It took me five minutes on the internet one morning in India for the penny to drop. One video led to another, until I came across undercover filming in factory farms, where farmers clubbed and threw chemically-fed chickens around the yard, where pigs were trapped in pens together with nowhere to move, separated from their young and castrated, where cows were branded in wire cages.

I realised that buying meat from a supermarket or a McDonald's directly supported this inhumanity. Kids are enticed by McDonald's because they and their parents are fed cleverly marketed phrases like 'happy meal'. If they knew of the barbaric nature of the production of the chicken nuggets involved in such a meal, they wouldn't touch them. There is nothing happy about fast food chains and the food they produce.

I turned vegetarian there and then. I came back from India and told Vanessa. The eating of meat is the done thing as an Englishman, even more so as a Yorkshireman. Up until this time I had been inclined towards the customary choices: 'meat and two veg', 'chicken and pasta', 'tuna and mayonnaise', 'fish and chips', the comfort food I had been brought up on.

I had to start thinking outside of the box, to read about food and learn about cultures and ways of cooking that supported a vegetarian diet. I started to find new and exciting foods that were readily available. Sometimes, when I eat out with people, I know they feel sorry for me because I haven't got meat on my plate, like it is a sacrifice or a hardship, or some kind of fad diet that I am undertaking.

I am often asked, 'what do you actually eat?' or 'where do you get your protein?' Many people don't think that a vegetable stir fry, or a lentil dahl made with amazing flavours and spices (one of the most popular Indian dishes), or quinoa porridge, can be tasty.

After a while I realised that nearly every single time humans eat meat, they garnish, cook or add tasty sauces to it and there is almost no exception to this rule. Even bacon, which many say is the tastiest meat, gets ketchup added to it. Hardened meat-eaters admit that chicken is average tasting at best without being barbecued, smothered in gravy or sauce, or fried in batter. Perhaps meat isn't as tasty as we think it is.

I feel strongly about it but I don't judge and hope not to be self-righteous. I don't feel I am on higher ground, it is simply how I chose to carry on. I am sure I own a garment of clothing derived from an animal source which makes me a resounding hypocrite!

At the British Open in 2009 I did a promotional campaign for PETA, the animal rights' campaigners. The slogan was: 'Squash obesity. Go veg!' My comments afterwards might have seemed heavy-handed but I felt they had to be. When people ask me why I don't eat animals, I tell them that I like chickens and cows and pigs in the same way that I like dogs and cats and that I don't like the thought of them being treated badly in order for me to eat them.

I feel even more of a responsibility as an athlete to prove that a vegetarian diet can aid rather than hinder athletic performance. There are numerous examples of successful athletes in different sports with either vegetarian or even vegan diets. Carl Lewis, one of the great Olympians, lived on a vegan diet during most of his career. Despite the fact that I have been very successful since becoming a vegetarian, people always seem eager to question the choice. I won the Tournament of Champions in New York eating vegan food and have endured some heavy periods of squash in my time eating in this way.

However, if I lose a match, I am forced to listen to comments about me 'needing some meat', or that I'm looking weak or pale. When I eat the varied and healthy diet that I do, and feel as good as I do, it is frustrating that people are so taken in by the meat myth, a myth perpetually propelled by the limitless propaganda all around us which promotes its consumption as normal and necessary. People rarely talk about the bad side of meat: the saturated fat content, or how little extra nutritional value it actually provides for instance.

It is a subject which I am asked about regularly and therefore I feel justified in talking about it. In conclusion, I will answer the three questions I am often asked. There is more to my diet than rabbit food. No, my girlfriend didn't force me to be a vegetarian. No, I definitely don't miss steak.

12 April 2010

The time has come to start behaving like an athlete again after two weeks of leisure and so, because it is Monday, it's back to work. Leisure means I eat what I want, I drink at will and I only train if I have the desire. After such over-indulgence I find that the desire to return to work often kicks in quite quickly; one can only feel a slob for so long. I have tried to keep going a little – these few weeks could only ever have been brief; the European Team event is just a few weeks away, and there is a break in the PSA calendar – and getting back into training after doing absolutely nothing is too painful, and mentally crushing.

I woke up feeling low. Low because I am overweight and have not exercised and even lower because Vanessa and I are at odds. The crux of the issue is that she would like children and I am doubtful, pondering far too deeply on the consequences. She is 34 and can't hold it off forever for an indecisive and selfish boyfriend who is all wrapped up in hitting a little black ball around.

She gently listens as I put my points across and tell her I can barely look after myself. She has made no attempt to force things, but the earnest look in her eyes shows unequivocal torment.

Our positions are misaligned. I wouldn't choose to have kids but I don't want to lose Vanessa. The issue has taken the wind from our sails for some time now.

Ironically, in the year I won five tournaments in a row in 2008, to date my most successful concentrated period of squash, I strongly recall the total despair I was feeling at the time regarding our relationship. On a Ryanair flight to

Sweden I hit miserable depths (I couldn't put this down solely to travelling Ryanair), intermittently running to hide in the bathroom, trying to avoid the other players who were on the plane. So vivid a low point was this that I could turn nowhere, not even to Vanessa, and even now I am baffled as to how I played so well at the time. People say that personal troubles have a great bearing on a professional life, but for those few weeks the distraction of getting ready for matches, of giving me something concrete on which to fix my mind, was a massive relief. I somehow managed to block out all my anxieties and worries for the duration of each match and I couldn't stop winning. I have rarely been more unhappy.

* * *

It could be squash's equivalent to the Steffi Graf-Andre Agassi romance, except I am yet to emulate Agassi. Vanessa Atkinson, like Graf, has stood at the top of the world in her sport. Like Graf, she is elegant, assured and has a continental way about her, which could be a result of the Anglo-Dutch upbringing: she was born in Newcastle and moved to Holland when she was nine, only leaving for England when she met me.

My similarities to Agassi are few: I have not been to the top of the world in my sport (just yet), I don't wear wigs (just yet) and I haven't taken crystal meth. Squash couples aren't rare and it is not difficult to see why: interests are shared and the players spend enough time together on tour to cultivate a relationship. Many of the men say they wouldn't be able to handle a relationship with a girl in squash but I have never understood such closed thinking. They say they feel the need to 'get away' from squash at home and that they are grateful for a diversion from the game. They seem to think that this is more likely if they don't have a squash girlfriend.

Vanessa and I do find other things to talk about besides squash, but I have to say, and I hope it has been the same for her, that when I do have a bad time on court she is willing to listen and talk to me and understands the difficulties having been through it all herself. She is well versed in what a squash player's life involves: frequent travel, long absences and selfishness.

It was at the Hong Kong Open in 2006 that we first came into contact. Before then we had barely noticed each other to say hello. After the initial meeting that night, I had enough balls to call her a week or so later (which apparently suitably impressed her – a text would have been a cop-out, she later told me).

We both ended that month dismally: Anthony Ricketts and me in Pakistan, and Vanessa at the World Open in Belfast where, seeded No 2, she lost in the second round. Ricketts and I had been holed up in an Islamabad hotel room for a week, jet lagged after travelling straight from America, each day ordering 'extra cooked' rice so as to make sure we wouldn't get food poisoning and living off minibar dairy milk chocolate, waiting for a bomb to drop somewhere or other. All I wanted was to see the fiery Dutch redhead with whom I had been exchanging messages on a computer screen.

I nearly lost to a 17-year-old Pakistani junior in what must surely have been the most tempestuous display of my professional career, during which I did everything short of killing the referee, believing him to have conspired against me. Everything in my head seemed to be contorted, and the contrast between being in Pakistan and being at home and meeting the temptress was so great that I just wanted to leave.

Not allowed to go out of the hotel there, we both snuck out across the road to the petrol station to buy some snacks, in what was the highlight of our week. We were both that tired in the evenings that I remember taking videos of Ricketts falling asleep on the bed at 6:30pm, and to counteract the tiredness we literally had to stand up and pace the room. With nothing but ourselves for entertainment, it was painfully tough to simply stick to the new time zone.

So desperate were we by the end of the week to get out of the place that, having both lost on the same evening, we took it in turns to plead with British Airways staff on the phone to ensure we were on a flight home. Ricketts was so hell-bent on getting back to England that I recall him snapping violently at his girlfriend, Shelley. Luckily we both bagged places on the next flight, and doubly fortunately, we found there was only a small charge to upgrade to business class, which we took gratefully. Feet up, I can never recall having felt so good to be sipping champagne at the front of an aircraft cabin.

I met Vanessa properly for the first time since Hong Kong after arriving home that night, elated to be in Leeds and not Islamabad. We spent the night in bars with fellow England player Jenny Duncalf and Ricketts, and got on well during the first weeks. Our relationship is very strong in my eyes, and I feel fortunate that Vanessa is part of my life. I hope I can be as loving and supportive to her as she is to me.

Flashback
1 April 2006
The Commonwealth Games, 2006, Melbourne.

Excitement, intensity, disappointment. It is the experience of a lifetime. The event in which people come together to celebrate sport – a place where the sun shines every day, and where a community engages with collective fervour to host the most memorable month's sporting action – is a huge success. There is a friendly feel and volunteers, athletes and spectators embrace this spectacular festival. The event suggests to me it is not all about the actual sport itself, the winning and losing of it. It is about far more than that. Everywhere I go, adorned in England clothing, wearing my accreditation, people speak. Without the accreditation and the kit, little notice is paid, but the labelling which tells people that YOU are part of the Commonwealth Games, gives people a licence to connect. To them we are important.

The Aussie people are friendly: 'How are you doing? Can we have a photo? Good luck!' This is the reception I get from people I have never met, when I walk towards the athletics stadium one balmy evening.

An hour before my quarter-final with Nick I go out for a walk: they line up outside the squash centre, queuing for tickets for miles before the session. I can scarcely believe my eyes. Are they all queuing to watch squash? The public turn up in their thousands. I lose but I win a silver in the doubles with Vicky Botwright. I find a great temporary cure for my lack of self-confidence by putting a Commonwealth medal around my neck.

Peter Nicol wins two golds, his singles effort is the highlight of not just his career, but most of his team-mates' careers. An unbelievable, thrilling, amazing occasion and I do not use those words lightly. Peter is like I have never seen him before on a court: he walks on for the introductions in the most relaxed fashion, smiling and waving. By the end he is a raging bull, celebrating, fist-pumping, possessed. That performance hardly got an acknowledgement in wider media circles. It should be recognised as a defining moment of a generation. It is a performance which ranks among the greatest sporting occasions many of us have ever seen. In any sport.

To celebrate the medals we go to Federation Square. We

make speeches, smoke cigars. Some of us are tearful. I do some commentary for the BBC, going to their makeshift studios in town for the semis and finals: a perk of being knocked out the round before. I meet a couple of student girls doing work experience in the offices there. I walk to the commentary box and the producer tells me the girls were rooting for me in my quarter-final. 'I think they took a shine to you' he says. All I can think is: 'are they insane?'.

Flattered, I get their numbers later in the week, mentioning the final party that we had planned, insinuating a possible meeting. All I feel is fear.

In a terrible mix up I drink too much at the team bar, and text them to meet up somewhere before going on to a casino. They are sober as judges. They get in to a taxi with me but I can tell they are thinking much less of me now. Where is my medal when I need it? I invite them to come with me and they decline, quite politely mumbling something about having to be somewhere else quite soon. They take one look at me and leg it. I must have been in a dreadful state, and added to a lifelong ineptness with any new relationship, my awkwardness descends to new, embarrassing levels. This disaster symbolises the beginning of the 'Commonwealth crash', the depressing period after this trip, and how I am far too useless to charm girls. It isn't my thing and it never has been. Why on earth I think I can be any better with a girl as a Commonwealth Games participant/commentator I have no idea. Who the hell do I think I am? Maybe I get too confident, what with the last few scintillating weeks, and the alcohol ingestion. They were the ones chasing me for once and tonight I am more ungainly and graceless than I can remember ever being.

Despite my effort at 'pulling', I spend the rest of the evening in the casino with friends who have flown over for the Games. At about 3am I start to wonder why I booked straight out of Melbourne the next morning, all of a sudden contemplating the fact that my flight leaves in six hours. I make a few calls to the airline from the casino to try to change my flight but I have no luck, and so I carry on drinking, conjecturing that going to bed at this stage would be both unnecessary and unhelpful.

Arriving back at the village at 6am I am confronted with the thought of packing my bags in a strongly inebriated state and boarding a bus to the airport, prior to two flights of fifteen and seven hours respectively in which my large frame would be compressed for the duration.

I arrive in LA. Everything is so different. Fat security women shout at me for my passport. I nearly give them my accreditation, that ticket to everything in Melbourne – free food, free transport, access to games venues, even respect – realising all of a sudden it is obsolete. A bit like me right now. I am merely another person at another airport, alone. The love, the respect, the friendliness and camaraderie has gone. I sit in a café waiting for the next flight. I text the Aussie girl, half apologising for my apparent laddishness. After six weeks of this rapture, I am isolated, and nobody here knows or cares about the Commonwealth Games. Why would they? They like baseball.

I think of my solitude, I think of my dad. I think of my mum. Now is the time I would ring her. I am about to embark on the biggest comedown of my sporting life so far.

I am relieved to get to Bermuda, hardly a bad place for a Games comedown. I check in to the Fairmont hotel in Hamilton with weary legs and a heavy head; I can scarcely remember having travelled in such brutal fashion; admittedly this was not helped by the all-nighter, and due blame must be apportioned to myself. The season is turning into quite a back-breaker even so; November and December yielded four major tournaments back to back, a first in my career. I arrive in Bermuda listless.

As is customary in Bermuda, I hire a scooter to get around the island and drive to one of the bays in the south. I park up, and find rocks. I sit for a while on one, looking out to the limitless crystal clear blue waters of the ocean, with the sun screaming and the wind talking. I sit on my rock to contemplate. As it did in LA and New York, reality hits me hard again, a feeling that is heightened by the setting and the solitude. I look back on the Games period, a whirlwind of emotion, sharing and togetherness. Scarcely a moment has been spent alone, and now I contrast that to the time and solitude that stands before me.

After winning events, I had always expected to feel immensely happy, and of course to a certain extent I do (whenever I win one), but the immediate aftermath is really quite strange. After the photos and the cameras, the interviews and the people, the only obvious thing to do is retreat to the hotel, usually alone, unless I have somebody with me. I look at the trophy, and the room, and it is odd. I wonder what on earth I should be doing next. It is a curious notion, where a human goes from a heightened environment, an environment of adulation and attention, to one where he is absolutely alone.

A couple of days later my Aussie friend Anthony Ricketts arrives in Bermuda. We eat room service together, remaining relatively inconspicuous to the outside world. We practise so badly for the week that we might as well not bother. At 9pm each night we watch 24 on the DVD player. Within the first 10 minutes I find myself stifling sleep and snorting. This goes on for days, when normally it would subside after a few good nights' sleep. Ricketts can't believe it. I tell him it's the night out, followed by the awful journey. I sleep long and well for days. I lose to Shabana in four tight games in the quarters. Time to go home.

FLASHBACK
January 1999

It was wet, dark and dreary. The weather could have no more reflected such an awful day if it had tried. I revelled unaware and at liberty as I trained after school at Pontefract Squash Club, which I often did in the evenings. This was to be a different evening, though, one after which things would change forever; an evening that would clinically wipe out a certain innocence I had for good.

I came off court, and Dad took me aside. 'James, your mum's had some results back. I think you should go home and see her.'

I don't remember what else was said between us but I had understood the implications. I do remember the feeling I experienced as I heard Malc sensitively tell me the news that my mother, Lesley, was – after months of speculative hospital visits to various specialists – seriously ill with cancer.

In a very odd way I almost expected it. I have often heard it said that 'cancer is something you expect someone else to get.' Well, this was not the case for me. I have always been in touch with death, part of that negative sensibility I have, a slight inclination towards having a glass that is half empty, and remember as a child dreading the moment of my parents' death. I had considered it, almost rehearsed it and so I was probably as ready for this news as much as Mum herself was. In any case, she had been having tests since the summer on the ominous lumps she had noticed in her neck, and so the thought of cancer had been considered.

I was strangely ready for it, but nothing could quite have prepared me for the consequence of being told for certain that it was true. In reaction to my Dad's faltering announcement over the balconies of court one and two, my heart sank, tightened as if it was overrun by electricity, and its only coping mechanism was to beat so fast that it hurt.

I couldn't drive and so Stan, a close friend, gave me a lift while my dad finished his Thursday night squash coaching. Nothing was said between us about Mum in the car. I'm sure he knew, but he was a man and I was an adolescent. We both knew it would be an impossible subject to broach, so we talked as men do. I suppose it must have been difficult to know how to react to a 15-year-old boy who had just found out that his mother was seriously ill.

I entered the house with such a deep feeling of shock, sadness and great trepidation that I barely knew what I was supposed to do. I opened the door to the living room and saw her look, a new look that was to be perceptible only during the two years that she suffered from cancer; a haunted and melancholy gaze visible only during this new chapter in our lives.

She glanced at me almost as if she was displeased to see me. I knew this could not be true; it was a raw expression of the deep turmoil that had so wretchedly and suddenly taken a hold of her.

Lou, her friend from work, sat beside her on the sofa but I barely registered her. I held my glance with my dear mother, confused and desperate; that look, a look on the face of a person who now stared deep into the unknown. My own face must surely have mirrored hers – and together, to Lou, we must have seemed like two people gripped by the most extreme fragility, loss and desperation. I said nothing, and within a few seconds had swallowed my mum in to my arms and we both sobbed unashamedly.

What on earth do we do now?

As the evening passed by, we began to realise that life as

we had known it had been a series of mostly comparatively happy moments, where we spent time and energy in a circus of trivial pursuits, like playing squash, doing school work or laundry, all of which we thought mattered. Of course now none of it really mattered. I felt trapped in a vacuum, detached from all the world.

Time, of course, in these situations, still passes and therefore something has to happen, and it did. I look back now and wonder how it was possible to do anything, or to carry on in any meaningful way in the immediate aftermath of such a revelation. As human beings, and it is a curious process, we somehow find ways to do so.

Being typically English, we went for the kettle and had tea, and this sounds absurd, but finding ourselves in such a sorrowful and desolate position, one of the only natural things to do was to look forward to small, sociable pleasures and drinking tea was strangely soothing. The mere mention of putting the kettle on was enough to ever so slightly allay a situation that was too painful to bear.

Everybody came around that night. I spoke to David and Lee, my two brothers, and my dad arrived after work and offered to stay. Each new face through the door brought a fresh set of tears and a fresh cup of tea.

It was clear that Mum didn't know what to do. She stopped work immediately and I stayed away from school for several days. There were no smiles for days, even weeks, and if we came close the thought was soon overcome by regret; to even think of smiling at such a time felt wrong.

Mum had learned that she had stage three ovarian cancer. The disease had spread to her neck and lymph nodes, and had it not shown itself in her neck then she would never have known. Ovarian cancer is labelled 'the silent killer' because it is very difficult to detect unless it manifests itself as a secondary elsewhere, which it did in her case, only rather late.

It suggested that the cancer hadn't been caught early, and so the prognosis was far from good. Still, at least she finally knew what the illness was. She had first found the lumps, and had felt constantly tired in the summer of 1998; it had taken too long to reach this stage.

I remember stirring in my sleep the following morning faced with that awful moment upon wakening, where the mind attempts to grapple with facts, somewhere in between actual reality and the dreamlike state which follows sleep. In seconds, the mind came to its senses, and deftly assimilated exactly what was going on. I realised it was true. It was time to face the day, and my poor mum, who I could hear downstairs.

This felt bad for me. God only knows what she had been through overnight. I ambled downstairs to find her folding clothes, which looked wrong.

'What are you doing that for? Sit down, relax.'

'I want to keep doing things.'

I put the kettle on.

She had many friends and was an extremely popular and likeable person. They gave her a great deal of strength and it helped her to adjust to living with the sentence she had received.

She knew she had to have a hysterectomy as a matter of urgency, and this was the first hurdle to overcome. This operation took place the following week, and sapped her physically. After a period of recovery she began her chemotherapy treatment.

The next 18 months would be a story of very many lows and one or two very precious highs. It was 18 months made up of waiting for test results, or hoping and praying for positive outcomes to scans; building up to the specialist's next visit, or hoping to hear of a good blood count. It would be a time of striving to find a positive outlook and being partly successful, only to be knocked back by a wall of negatives. All the while, nobody really knew how successful it had been, and as far as I am aware very little progress has been made on the treatment of ovarian cancer. The doctors, we all felt, were stabbing in the dark, and it was so very frustrating and draining.

Indeed, it wasn't all bad. It is fascinating how the human body can absorb, and then react positively to pain and suffering. Mum had cancer for the entire 18 months up until her death, but once she became resigned to the fact and could adapt, she very much made the most of her time. She attended parties and social occasions, living life as fully as she was able, and at times we didn't think about the cancer. She often looked healthy, vibrant and intermittently, she was undoubtedly happy.

FOUR

TIME TO PLAY FOR THE TEAM

27 April 2010

Arrived in Aix-en-Provence for the European Team Championships. Up until now my squash has thrived in team events, even though I am probably less suited to a team environment than some.

Teams like to go around in groups, wear uniforms and pretend to like each other. I am distinctly repelled from any kind of group, don't suit uniforms, and struggle to like myself. It is not my way to express outward feelings of togetherness with Vanessa, my long-suffering companion, or my dad or my brother, the closest people to me, let alone a team, especially if they're forced, and expressions of unity that are entirely forced seem all wrong. Nevertheless, despite a natural aversion to this environment, I think the teams I have played with recently have operated in a balanced way: being English and generally more stoical than our rivals, we have conducted ourselves with a tempered unity; we have gone about our business, concentrating on each individual rather than worrying about 'team spirit' to the extreme. I'm not sure I believe in such a thing, but I realise that people want to believe in such a thing. It's a buzz phrase. People like positive buzz phrases.

The French, for instance, go about beating their chests and making exclamations worthy of a 15th century battlefield, despite not liking each other. Donning the French tracksuits changes things completely for them. Their chests are positioned slightly further forward than usual.

In squash – and many may disagree with this – there is little point in worrying about team spirit too much. I have shared success with players over the years that I wouldn't call friends; I know it is not sport, but Keith Richards and Mick Jagger were never the best of friends, nor were Pete Townshend and Roger Daltrey. It didn't seem to stop millions thinking of them as shaping the entire landscape of music. My best win in an England shirt came at the World Team Championships in 2005. Everyone went on about the team spirit. I thought there was none. Fellow Yorkshireman Lee Beachill and I didn't talk to each other all week, and I went about my business inconspicuously, not enjoying Islamabad and constantly dreaming of home. I played brilliantly to beat world champion Shabana in the first rubber, leaving Peter Nicol to clear up for a comfortable win. Team spirit didn't come in to it.

I have found all too often that coaches, the public, or masters of ceremonies, like to label players 'friends', or talk up 'team spirit'. It sounds good, it's a clean, bright thing to say, but often it is unfounded and has been presumed because of reasons of geography. Most of the players are not best of friends, and quite often squash players get along worse with their countrymen. I am quite sure this is the case with France (certainly Thierry Lincou and Greg Gaultier, their top players, haven't had the smoothest of relationships) and the Egyptian team members who won the World Team Championships in 2009 may not have been on one another's birthday card lists. I'm not saying it's all warfare, but it is very difficult for everybody to be friendly.

The sun is shining in Aix. As always at the European Championships there is a healthy and sociable atmosphere around the place, quite different from the PSA events. Every year club standard players mix with the best players in the world, and the tournament provides a platform for players from countries such as Luxembourg or the Isle of Man to compete in the same event as France and England.

I missed it last year and I'm glad to be back. It is hugely positive that the sport continues to stage events like this, gathering all sorts of different nations and standards and it speaks volumes for the game. Golf, or tennis, or football will never be able to stage events in this vein and for all the sport's lack of money and shortcomings, this is to its credit. Happily squash has remained down to earth, transportable and accessible.

The tournament is being played in the busiest, sweatiest, rabbit warren like club I have played in, but it has great old fashioned character and is charming. A gorgeous pool area stands within the squash club grounds, where the teams assemble, frolicking half naked during short periods of down time.

As a team, we have been encouraged to be vociferous and to sit in the 'team corner' when we can. Perhaps I'm just miserable, or perhaps I prefer the quiet way, but a silent team can win if the players are good enough. I'm all for shouting, encouragement and support, but not if it is done gratuitously, or for a show of togetherness. I don't mean to be overly derogatory. Ever an individual, I am still a team player. But I don't go in for all the team bonding thing. All five players in our team are different. The best thing to do is to work with that in mind. Our present team does it well I think.

As usual on Europeans final day, exhaustion set in. We beat the French again to win. Thierry and I played cat and mouse for 100 minutes and, because of my relative lack of condition (I have been fitter), I nearly died on there. On first, in front of a fiery and boisterous French crowd, I came from 2-1 down to win. I had forgotten how gratifying it was to silence a French crowd, especially as my dialogue with the referee in the fifth had only seemed to increase the intensity of their chanting, against which my pleas could not be heard.

On striking a crisp winning ball, I became a team player all of a sudden, all patriotic, one of the lads, saluting the England bench proudly. I was fragile, though, having been in physical trouble as early as the second game. It is hardly the greatest sign to be struggling to absorb oxygen as early as game two. But I was thrilled to win the rubber for England on another important occasion.

2 May 2010

Went to watch the World Snooker final at the Crucible, Sheffield with Vanessa. It was Neil Robertson against Graeme Dott, two vastly different characters, and a world away from any team environment. I love the psychology of snooker, everything quiet. It is like a sizzling cauldron of intensity, a test of who can hold it together the best under scrutiny and pressure.

5 May 2010

I wake up wondering whether to train, hoping that a chest infection I picked up a couple of days ago might have cleared. It hasn't. Malcolm, David and I are heading for some exhibitions in Norfolk and Edinburgh, but my heart isn't in it. I decide to train in Sheffield with Mark and press on. I arrange for Malcolm and David to pick me up from Sheffield.

The training went well; we stayed on the weights and strength work so as not to over exert the breathing and the hour's work prevented me wallowing in self-pity. My mind escaped all thoughts of the cold. I coughed again on the way down, but refreshed and rejuvenated from the training, and in the car, engaging heartily in conversation with Malc and David, I found myself differently disposed from this morning, when I had been so despondent that calling the whole trip off had not seemed unthinkable. Funny how things can turn around with a positive frame of mind. I am starting to sound like Mick, Mr Positive himself.

A meeting with Malcolm's old headmaster, in beautiful rural Norfolk, perked me up even more, especially when he served us with alcohol. Quite honestly, I had by this time forgotten all about the illness. Keeping busy and entertained had had a distinct effect on my ailments, and I was much encouraged by the fact that drinking a bottle of wine could have such a positive impact on my wellbeing. I wondered why I had not done this before and resolved in future to do it more often, having seen at first hand all the good it can do. It shows that scientists and doctors shouldn't always be believed. Wilde should really have said that alcohol, taken in sufficient quantities, can bring about all the effects of drunkenness and wellness.

It is an interesting notion that a positive mindset can stave off an illness. Positive thinking alone is not the cure for everything, but the old adage 'mind over matter' undoubtedly goes a long way.

15 May 2010

I arrived in Egypt and the reminders came thick and fast of that awful trip I had here in 2006 when I contracted acute gastroenteritis, ending up in hospital in Cairo. It was my first experience of the place.

Not great memories, I have to say, and I remain uncomfortable here. Despite an affection for some of the Egyptian players, it is one of my least anticipated trips.

It is impossible to eat with anything like a relaxed attitude. Water bottles have to be checked for unbroken seals (if the seal is broken, theoretically the hotel waiter could have filled the bottle up with tap water, and yes this can happen), ice from all food and drinks is avoided and anything uncooked and lukewarm is sent back. Salads are forbidden (they will most probably have been washed with tap water), and the water that is used (including for brushing teeth) must be from a bottle of mineral water. I am used to it because of the frequency of my visits to India, Pakistan and Egypt, but this vigilance in my eyes is wearisome, and the first shower back home is liberating, knowing the water won't kill you.

The general attitude here, whether it be from street hagglers or taxi drivers, is as abrasive as it is frustrating. Everything is won or lost. Very little is ever given, and nowhere is this truer than on the city roads. Every inch of space is taken by a car, and Egyptians don't do lanes or order. It makes a week in Cairo stressful.

I lost to Ramy 3-0 in the quarters. The match was tight but he was better at the business end of each game. I don't sleep after a loss unless I drink or take pills. It is therefore a good job Mick is here. In him I have a drinking partner. We talked until the early hours. He talked. I listened.

I feel flat after seeing Ramy's result against Karim Darwish, which read 3-0 in the latter's favour. After such a dominant performance last night, in which he nullified my strengths, I can't fathom a result like this, but in many respects it shows that no player is immune to a loss, even the world number one, and it confirms more than ever that different styles of player, when mixed, can produce varying results. Recent matches against Darwish have gone in my favour, yet last night Ramy demolished me only to lose to him easily.

The same happened in Qatar last year: Ramy again beat

me well, yet 24 hours later he struggled to hit the ball, Darwish winning that time 3-2. This is by no means a new phenomenon; the clashes of styles have always, and will always, lend suspense and excitement to sport.

Ramy's loss clears the way for Nick to become world No 1 this week. It will be the first time an Englishman has topped the rankings since Lee Beachill in 2005.

It is time to move on, anyhow, because ahead of me stretches a period of rest and relaxation. The time off is well needed. Tomorrow to London, to see my mate Charlie.

26 May 2010

Vanessa left today to go to the European Individual Championships, after joining me here for a few days in London. How glad I am I didn't play that event. A good decision for once. Having a brilliant few days in London, both on my own and with Vanessa. I saw *Oliver* with her last night in the West End; it is a new favourite and the second time improved it for me. The best shows, like the best films, are the ones seen more than once.

The talent and showmanship which is on display on the West End and Broadway continues to fascinate and enthral me. *Blood Brothers*, mine and Vanessa's last West End outing together after Canary Wharf was a sensation. To be visibly moved at the end of a show in which the lead is played by a Spice Girl is verging on embarrassment for most 27-year-old males, but Mel C was utterly compelling as Mrs Johnson.

I saw *Phantom of the Opera* on Wednesday for the second time and *Macbeth* at the Globe last night. I'm due to be out with Charlie tonight, to his favourite London haunt, where we'll be joined by our good mate John, so that we can all fall over together at the end of the night, 5:30am to be more precise. Two weeks ago I was a focused, fit athlete, hungry for victory. Now I am out of shape and bordering on alcoholism.

Everything to excess.

There'll be no more of this for six months once the training starts, so I'll enjoy it while it lasts.

30 May 2010

Bank holiday: a bad excuse for a day off, a three-day weekend, for which there is yet to be found a valid reason. From an athlete's point of view, bank holidays are hopelessly placed, and duly ignored; they do not usually correspond to the schedule, almost always coming at the wrong time (except for this one perhaps) and, if a big tournament is imminent, then work is obliged to be done, regardless of what everyone else does. Carrying on as normal is better anyway. Work is underrated.

I need to stop resting and do something. These periods of rest, lacking the usual training, are all well and good, but the pleasures aren't as pleasurable without the pain. The food doesn't taste as good, the beer does not have quite the same effect. I know I need to take the time off though.

I'll always remember reading an article on the trend in which athletes display tendencies to be superstitious, or even obsessive compulsive. The piece referred to the 'all or nothing' infirmity, which can be explained as the state of mind a person develops as a result of an extremely intense lifestyle, and the mental reaction to such a thing. This syndrome, or state of mind, is often inflicted by mental switches, in which a person's experiences flit from one extreme to the other. Athletes, artists, singers and actors can be particularly susceptible to it, and perhaps this explains why some are notoriously difficult to work with. It is all or nothing. Athletes' lives consist of great contrasts: from the hardest training session to hours in bed; large crowds to empty hotel rooms; World Championship finals to long periods of solitude. There is such a gulf in the level of intensity that for some it can cause problems.

Athletes will pursue their dream doggedly and incessantly for months on end, undertaking clean diets, little alcohol and no general vice whatever. When the period is over, when the occasion to which one has solidly built ceases, there is a let-down period consisting of holidays, relaxing, switching off. Each athlete has their own method of release. It is an extremely important passage of time, a time in which to recharge the batteries and rediscover bite and enthusiasm, which may or may not have been eaten away at during the tough build-up of the previous months.

After spending six months training, playing, watching everything I eat, and striving to be the very best at squash, I tend to find I am close to mental collapse. To counter this, I feel a rapacious urge to eat. All or nothing. People whose lives maintain a steady pace, with less intensity, and few of the highs and the lows, may not and mostly will not follow this path.

For me the drink is less of a problem than food; soon enough the hangovers repel any inclination to obliterate myself. All this seems to come from all the effort taken to do everything perfectly all year round; it swells up inside, and the mental explosion takes hold, manifesting itself, in my case, through extreme over indulgence.

I was interested to read that these scenarios are not uncommon in athletes, who are often so intensely focused. Athletes are driven by such incredible determination, and will to succeed, that the let down period is often also done in an absolute way, almost as intense to the opposite extreme, whether it be gorging on chocolate, downing 10 pints or staying in bed all day.

Disappointingly, but perhaps fortunately, none of the above can be done in great abundance as a squash player, and so when the time lends itself to doing so, I indulge all I can and want, simply because I can.

I feel that, destructive as these periods of excess are, and that I am made considerably rotund by their onset, they are absolutely necessary, allowing me to go again, to strive again in the knowledge that the system has had a reboot. Being obsessive about indulgence for a week or two allows me to be obsessive about squash once more.

I know I have a tendency to suffer from the extremes, or conversely needing them to exist! The highs and lows of playing a professional sport make it a struggle; the eating binges counteract the careful diet that I take during the year, making me chubby but giving me the let-down I need.

I pay great attention to detail to training and application to my work, and unfortunately for me this obsession filters through in to other areas of my life.

I cast my mind back to sometime around 1996. I am 13. I stand in the kitchen, preparing myself to go to bed, a process that has become distressing of late; it will be half an hour, at least, before I am in my bed.

The first ritual is the gas taps, and it is 'the check' that causes me the most problems. I check all four taps repeatedly, every night. Tonight I am not clear that they are all off. 1, 2, 3, 4, all off. I repeat this over and over out loud, to myself. It is the behaviour of a madman I know, the stuff that people laugh at when I tell them, in more relaxed moments. It has become far from funny now.

I walk out of the door, but I have to go back. I cannot be sure that the gas taps are all off so I decide to do my other checks. It may refresh my mind a little. I check behind the sofa, God only knows what for, and I check that the front and back door are locked. I look under the table. It is all a routine, the same checks every night. They evolve with time. Sometimes I create a new check to add to the list. I do all the other checks and complete them, but I am in quite a tangle with the gas taps, because the gas taps is the only 'check' behind which lies a real reason. Years ago, I stored the memory of seeing an advert on television about gas leeks in the home. This was etched on to a highly sensitive mind. The advert implored the viewer to be careful with gas, highlighting the dangers and this clearly stayed with me, doing me more harm than good.

The problem has become more complex than simply checking the gas taps are off. That part is simple. The problem I now have is that I am sometimes unable to trust my mind to tell me the gas is off, which is far more worrying and debilitating than just the 'check' itself. What was once a small problem is now spiralling out of control. Mum, upstairs and trying to sleep before her day's work, becomes frustrated, asking me more sternly to come to bed. Time rattles on and I can't complete the checks; she gets more angry, and I become increasingly upset knowing that I need the time. I know it is impossible for her to understand what is happening when I can barely understand it myself.

'James! Bed, now!' She is not happy, and she is coming downstairs.

'I can't. I just can't.'

As ridiculous as this may seem, I am on the verge of desperation, and I can hold it in no longer, fully realising how much this is taking out of me. We have laughed about it before, stating that it is purely one of my differences, my idiosyncrasies, but this time when she marches downstairs to see me crying on the kitchen floor she sees it too. Her voice softens slightly, but I hear undertones of incredulity.

'Come on James. Look, they are all off. ' She looks at them with me. 1, 2, 3, 4. All off. See? All off.'

I have to settle for this. I ask her again if everything is off, before joining her in her bedroom, perching on her bed. We talk it over, and both decide that she will help me each night, checking with me, holding my hand so to speak, and that if this doesn't work, then we will seek help.

My parents had seen an unusual maturity in me as a young child; I told my brother to speak properly at five and wore tweed jackets aged 12. Add this to the tendencies to feel low, and because of the independence I had been given as a child, that ever-present desire to be a little alone and occupy myself, and then the gradual filtering of the obsessive compulsive traits, I think they saw that they were dealing with a different child.

I don't say different to make myself sound special in the slightest, but I undoubtedly had an unusual capacity and as a child I was shy and uncool. There is no wonder I have a penchant for spending time in health shops and hoarding carrier bags.

Today I have learnt to control these tendencies, but they are all still there. Even though in the house I live in my kitchen hob runs on electricity, the taps still get checked. Presently though, and thank God, it doesn't blight my life in the way it did.

10 June 2010

It is my week off and I have been preparing for my brother David's wedding on Saturday, to Sarah Kippax, the England international. He has chosen myself and Lee, our oldest brother, to be his best men, which obviously requires the enormous undertaking of the speech. I have spoken in public at squash events regularly but this is a different thing altogether.

I was at first honoured to be David's joint Best Man. I

doubt he really knew what else to do, but the lead up to the event is now causing me to wonder why he has inflicted such a feeling of unease on me; the thought of having to sit there sweating all day, having to lay off the bottle until it is over, is filling me with great apprehension. Thankfully every time I have spoken to him during the course of the week he has sounded similarly stressed, which has lifted my spirits no end. I always feel better after talking to him and to know my only ordeal is the speech itself.

I have always found weddings hilarious occasions, where often non religious people subscribe to religious principles for a day without knowing why, and where those involved either get far too pissed, depressed, or fall out with each other. Parents and grandparents are often the most intriguing, looking and displaying intense pride, making it clear this is a highlight of their lives. I have never understood why parents are so happy for their children after they say their vows. They often cry with pride and happiness, but considering the amount of damage the whole big knees up causes to their bank balance, they should be crying in utter dismay.

Nevertheless, some weddings can be great fun, and are excellent for getting legless. I predict David and Sarah's wedding will be a good one, with a positive mix of characters due to attend. As long as the relatives get along nicely all will be well.

15 June 2010

Summer training and the first day of the yearly Colorado Camp in Estes Park and Boulder, an hour's drive from Denver. We have spent long and happy times here over the last years.

The idea was the brainchild of Damon Leedale Brown,

whom I have known since I was 16. Before 1996, there was no such thing as lottery funding, or any kind of subsistence support from Sport England. There was the national coach, the governing body, and that was it. Players had to make it on their own back then. From 1997 onwards, a central fund became available, taking England Squash, or the Squash Rackets Association as it was called then, from one extreme to the other. Suddenly money was available, and masses of it. Some young players were rumoured to be receiving £17,000 grants in one year. There was so much money, and the association had to find something to do with it.

Out of this funding came an influx of new staff. Suddenly we had regular national training camps, with psychologists, sport scientists, nutritionists and physiologists. When we played in England Team events, we were laughed at: there were more staff than players.

Damon appeared as a result of the funding; he was employed by the SRA as the lead strength and conditioning coach and his brief was to educate and oversee the training of the players who were part of the new World Class Performance Programme.

My first contact with him was over the phone: I had just reached the semi-finals of the British Junior Open in Sheffield and he rang to offer his support and advice. We ended up talking for half an hour about the correct things to eat leading up to matches and I suppose this was my first introduction to this alternative type of professionalism. I was already well suited to working hard and training, but I was about to learn about training techniques that at the time had stood outside the parameters of my squash knowledge. My relationship with Damon was about to flourish, and I was going learn how to train smart, and not always just hard. Damon was the catalyst.

As soon as I met Damon, I began working with him at squads and at home in greater depth. He was diligent and driven and would seek out times to come and visit Pontefract to do sessions there, rather than just wait for the squads. I was so committed to becoming good even back then that I intuitively knew I had to listen to him, despite much cynicism from some parties. Back in 1997, sports science was seen by many coaches as gobbledegook and many saw it as a threat. It was by no means considered in the way it is now: an entirely vital part of any athlete's plan.

I gradually built a close relationship with Damon. I look back on these years and realise now that the work Damon put me through was bracing me for 15 years playing world class squash. His intention was to instil strength in to my young legs and to nurture a constitution bestowed with limited athletic ability. Aged 16, I was weak, angular and uncoordinated and this period of my development was absolutely vital, though I didn't know it. Back then, I just liked Damon and loved his sessions.

Before parents of child prodigies start getting over ambitious, I must point out again that these years were not so important because I trained hard, but rather they were important because I trained cleverly. With such a lack of natural ability, this sensible work was vital for me and I would not be the same athlete now had I not done it.

I feel absolutely indebted to Damon for his consummate education and the time he so selflessly and passionately has given me. I learnt so much from his expertise, and was lucky to have met him. He taught me the principles of strength work and Olympic lifting, and how to engage in the exercises properly, specifically and safely. I learnt from him the importance of training the core muscles. I never once did a bench press or an arm curl with Damon; every single exercise was done for a reason, and that reason directly related to becoming a better squash player.

When he was shunted from the ranks of England Squash

in 2003, he found a way to maintain our relationship whilst taking on another job at Sheffield Hallam University, never asking for a penny from me in the process. His passion was to improve players and to work with them hands on, not to milk money out of them, and he knew he wasn't going to give up on me after all the hard work. Above everything, I always knew he cared, and every result of mine, now and then, nods to his work with me over the years.

After moving to the US in 2005, Damon phoned me early in 2007 to discuss his ideas for the camp in Boulder, Colorado. He had a contact for a family who ran a training centre by the name of 'Active at Altitude' of which he had learned from friend and British marathon runner Liz Yelling. He said it was beautiful, in the Rocky mountains, and was a triathlete's and marathon runner's heaven. He explained his idea, and I feared that I wouldn't need much more convincing.

Terry and Jacqui Chiplin, who own the house and feed the campers, are perfect hosts and have become very good friends. Perched in the most serene and beautiful area, the house overlooks elegant snow-capped mountains and the only distraction is the sound of a prairie dog or a rustling squirrel.

The wake up is early, 6:35am, and the first session comprised an early morning run in Boulder, one of America's less conservative cities, 50 minutes away from Estes Park.

It feels good to be back here again in this spectacular part of the world, although adapting to the 9,000 feet of altitude is difficult. I felt nauseous after the run; I am lacking fitness and the tiredness from the travel, together with the altitude, brought about a shocking feeling. Perhaps being fat didn't help either.

In the afternoon Damon had scheduled our return to the Flatirons Athletic club in Boulder. On entering, it feels as if one is in some kind of boot camp for health freaks. Everyone here is fit, toned, muscular and super healthy, and the feeling is infectious. Boulder, as a city, exudes a sense of health and well being; there are no fat people in Boulder, making it almost the antithesis of the archetypal American city.

Damon took us through a good warm-up and some light routines. I had done enough after an hour and a half, so took myself out of the rest of the session. It was only ever going to be a light day today, I was sure of that.

The evenings are glorious here, back at Terry and Jacqui's retreat. The food was ready on our return from training and we duly gobbled it up, feeling that lovely tired feeling after training. We talk and enjoy the food before sleep, and we will be ready to go again tomorrow. Vanessa and I, despite our regular visits, never fail to feel incredibly fortunate to be here.

17 June 2010

The altitude is severe. The air is thinner as the altitude increases meaning there is less oxygen to breathe than at ground level. Depending on the level of altitude, the effects vary enormously. I suffer from sickness and headaches during the first week, a common ailment. Simply climbing a flight of stairs brings about a feeling of breathlessness, and at first this is alarming. Even more shocking is waking in the middle of the night in the midst of a desperate attempt to inhale, in such a way that it feels as if I might be having a heart attack.

After time spent living and training at altitude, the body adapts to the change in oxygen density, therefore altitude training is a popular choice for elite athletes; if they time it to lead into competition at sea level, theoretically speaking they should feel very comfortable with the change in oxygen density.

Second day in, and we readied ourselves for the first mountain bike ride of the camp, the first of four. It is a spectacular ride among the mountains, and despite being constantly starved of oxygen and in dire pain after the climbs, the occasional regroup gave us a chance to stare in absolute wonder at the scenery.

The Rocky Mountains are one of nature's gifts to humankind, and with all respect to have spent my life training in Pontefract, I do consider myself very lucky to be able to come out here to 'work'. At home my view from the gym is of the town's cemetery; here in Boulder it is of snow-capped mountains which are normally only seen through the canvas of an expensive painting. There are times, though, when the pain of the training blots out the beauty of the scenery, to the point where I couldn't care less how pretty the hills are.

A solid warm-up was followed by down wall practices with targets for 40 minutes. Then came a strength movement circuit, where I really started feeling it. Two stations did ghosting to one corner, the other two did backward and forward lunge, and one leg squat, both with dumbbells. The second circuit was to ghost the other two corners, and the lunges were a side lunge followed by a cross lunge with dumbbell repeated, and a corkscrew with dumbbell or weight. Condition games followed to finish.

Ghosting is a classic squash drill, one where you learn the art of moving around the court without the ball. It trains the muscles to move in the most specific way for squash.

The session today written down wouldn't seem like a great deal normally, but I am spent. Coming here still carrying a spare tyre was not the most sensible move, but there was little option, the season going on for so long. It's substantially tougher than last year, when I was fit after the rehab from my op. It's a dreaded run around Fern lake tomorrow morning. Bed calls.

* * *

On the drive to the trail I feel nervous; half excitement, half dread. Training is the most natural thing in the world, yet I am sometimes scared to death of it.

Today it scares me even more. Not only because it is training but it is running. Heavy-boned six footers weren't meant to run. I know it will be painful, and I know I will go through with it, so there is no escape.

Pain is unavoidable if success is the required result at a world level. It would be easy to duck out, hang back, only run half. I could find an excuse. But then that is a mental weakness, which would undoubtedly make me less good than I could be.

I cannot live with that. Even though I would like to, I tend not to cut corners, and this is a trait that is essential in all world class performers. The people who say they 'could have been' or 'should have been' world class tend to lack this mental ability.

The part before, the application of sun cream or the fixing of the bandana, or the tying of the shoelaces, is almost the hardest part. Before I know it we are off and running.

It's OK for now, but there is a brutal mile and a half climb coming up to get to the top, at 8,000 feet. I hear breathing and pattering of footsteps behind me as I concentrate on the rocks and how best to dodge and weave them. It's Damon, who goes ahead to take some photos and when I reach him he says 'good work, James', though I'm already finding this hard enough that I don't bother acknowledging him. I know he finds it funny when I don't talk to him, which makes me more unresponsive. From this point on it will get steeper and harder and Damon, once the rest of the group has passed him, will try to catch me up. He loves the competition, and his light frame helps him to run very well.

Maybe I'm going too fast here. I hit a couple of 20-yard inclines which are so steep they take my breath away. The oxygen deficit hits me; soil falling over my head. Rocks everywhere. Must be quick with the footwork. I feel like an oaf. Here we go. Pain.

It starts to feel harder to breathe, the inclines are now so ridiculous that I can barely walk up them, let alone run. I mean this; I can hardly run. Maybe I went too fast to start. Several times I seem to be on the precipice, reaching the limits of my aerobic capacity. I hear feet and breath. Christ, Damon already.

'Maybe ease off the gas a bit James. You went off so fast. There is still a fair bit of climbing to do.'

I don't talk but at the end of that incline I stop, which I hate doing. I never stop! I went far too fast. Perhaps I should be a little sensible considering I am only a week in to the altitude and 10 days ago I was overweight. Each time I look up there is another hill and I am always looking at the soles of Damon's shoes, or the next rock. These images on which I focus are almost symbolic of the hurt, but give me something to focus on. Every time I look at the letters A-S-I-C-S on Damon's shoes, I want to cry.

I make a stop or two, but I push and push until we reach the top. I drive my arms to try to get me up the inclines, but my whole body is so tired. I have never felt such tiredness in my upper body; it has seized emphatically.

Getting to the top means that the rest of the five-mile run (I know it doesn't sound much) is mostly downhill, but this still requires concentration and skill, despite being aerobically easier than the inclines. There is a strong footwork element involved, and the body must decelerate efficiently coming down, so it can be more challenging on the joints and limbs.

There is some flat at the end of the trail which seems to go on and on, and I am starting to feel awful, different to just plain tired. I stop again, wobbling. God knows what is wrong; I never stop. Maybe I went in to such a hard run prematurely, not having acclimatised properly to the conditions. My body is failing me, understandably so. I lie on the floor, gulping sports drink. Depleted and exhausted, an overwhelming urge to sleep has come over me which must mean I am about to faint. I have never ever felt the need to sleep in the direct aftermath of a session.

I manage not to pass out there and then, but head straight back to Terry's and sleep soundly for a couple of hours. I may have overdone it today.

25 June 2010

The day of death. Hill sprint day. The same place, Chautauqua Park, is the venue for the hill sprints every year, a beautiful space overlooking the Flatirons mountains in Boulder.

The session looks like child's play on paper: it consists of nine sprints. Not a lot. At the end of the session, because of the intensity of each set, those who have pushed hard are simply ruined, bereft of the merest drop of energy.

We do an 80 metre sprint with a decent incline, a 200 metre sprint with a more pronounced incline, and a final sprint of about 350 metres with a horrible incline. This is repeated three times. I try to think how best I can describe the utter horror of the second two hill repeats, especially the longer one.

The warm-up is tough because of the onset of pure dread. We exchange words with each other, trying to be comical, thinking it might help, but there is little doubting our general acceptance of the fact that we are dying inside. I look at my pathetic Casio watch. It reads 10am. What I would give for it to be 11am. The first two repeats are hard but doable; the body, at such an early stage in proceedings, is fresh and equipped to take the punishment.

Damon and I crouch at the start position for the third rep, the long hill. To involve the 12 or so people on the camp to partake in this barbarism, the session is formatted by dividing the group into teams for relays. On this rep I am lined up with sadistic Damon. I am not as fast a runner, and so my aim is to stay with him. His is to fend me off. We were both born highly competitive – and it is not a competitiveness which stems from wanting to beat each other, but more an innate competitiveness which cannot be confined and drives one to complete such a physical challenge to the very best of one's abilities. Put it this way, it is not quite a race but it's not the sort of challenge either of us would saunter through.

We get the signal to drive away from our start position, and I swing my arms, feeling in the first few strides that my size is a hindrance. Come on legs, go! The shale type surface of the track makes it even more of a challenge for my oversized limbs. My feet are too big to handle the dry sand and my body is lumbering and uncoordinated.

I try to quicken the cadence of my legs and soon develop a lolling rhythm, a couple of steps behind the more greyhound-like Damon. I see my shadow on the track and think how awkward my running style seems. My legs are moving as fast as they can go. The initial climb is reasonable, but 25 or so seconds in comes a more steep incline, which is immediately registered: the lungs begin to falter, and the legs no longer pick up momentum on the drive. I go for the second phase. The terrain plateaus ever so slightly, but as I look up with a strained face, there is at least 70 metres left and a desperately steep-looking second incline to boot.

I just keep driving. As I hit the incline I feel a dreadful deficit. My legs are giving nothing whatever; bystanders must be thinking they are watching some kind of alternative running-on-the-spot freak show because I am not going anywhere. It is, after all, a public area, more used for leisurely walks than all-out hill efforts. My arms, like they did on the run just the other day, have tied up like never before. What is it with the arms seizing up all the time? It's akin to having an acute dose of pins and needles whilst drowning.

I drive my depleted arms and legs up the last few metres of this steep incline, despite a visible lack of forward motion, and I have been reduced to exhaustion within a minute and a half. I reach the rock, our stopping point, and have to extend my back so as to get my arm up in the air (this is our signal to team members at the start to begin their leg) but I have no thoughts for them. My mind doesn't work; it is shrouded in delirium, and it cannot rationalise a thing in the wake of this pain.

During the most brutal exercise we are rendered helpless and strange and it means that we can do almost anything we like. We can swear or shout, bump in to people and fall over: no one cares because of the pain, which is acknowledged by onlookers. Bizarre behaviour is forgiven.

At the end of the rep, as I endeavour to capture oxygen, I lack even the co-ordination or ability to collapse onto the floor. I would only roll back down the hill. So I stay upright, gasping for my life, undoubtedly grotesque looking to the jovial, vociferous Americans taking their morning stroll. After 25 excruciating seconds the breathing begins to slow ever so slightly and the pain begins to fade.

Many athletes are familiar with this feeling – digging to the bottom of the well – whereupon extreme physical limitations are reached. It makes sense for squash players to experience the sensation regularly during training, so they are adequately accustomed to it during a tough match. Many athletes are also used to feeling the sense of near-elation at completing such a tough session. This state of mind is reached for several reasons:

1. It is over. The next one is hopefully a couple of days away.
2. It enables you to eat more.
3. It is a session in the bank

These are the sessions which give an athlete his security at 9-9 in the fifth; that give him or her, at the very least, knowledge and confidence that he or she has been through this pain before, and come out of it. It is during these sessions that the rehearsal for the hardest periods of play on a squash court takes place; much like the many rehearsals of a cast in a play. Familiarity through hard work and repetition are the vital ingredients which lead to success. Perhaps these factors account for about 90 per cent of success. The other 10 per cent, I would suggest, is talent.

These sessions, those that are so mentally difficult, those that hurt so much, are the ones that can give colour and clarity to the wildest dreams or ambitions that I have of achieving great things in squash. These sessions make the dream a believable concept.

I feel indestructible and every athlete will know what I mean. Yes, sitting on a sofa or lying in the sun is always good but this post training feeling is comparable and probably in the end better. For me, pleasure and pain are always connected.

5 July 2010

The training has been interrupted by a week in New York with the kids at StreetSquash, an initiative aimed at helping the underprivileged gain access to the game. It has been borne out of the fact that the sport is entirely unavailable to kids on the street over here. Squash is still buried in its elitist grave, and it is hard to see many kids overcoming this without the work of StreetSquash. Presently, kids who play squash in America are almost exclusively from middle class backgrounds and their main objective is to gain access to a decent university.

There were some good moments over the week, some kids who were willing to listen and learn, and we hope we provided some inspiration for them. Many have difficult lives, far removed from comfort and familiarity, and bereft of any level of steadfastness, often going from foster parent to foster parent, and those who have parents can often find themselves, in a frightening role reversal, being the carer. One girl who was training on Thursday was looking a little tired and bored, and I was slightly unhappy with her commitment to the session. I asked Sage, the man in charge of our trip there, and he told me that her mother had just that day been sent to prison.

16 July 2010

How good it feels to be back in Pontefract. The welcoming smiles at the squash club of people I know can't be found in New York. It remains difficult to find a bean and quinoa salad in Pontefract, but people here don't slam doors in your face. Ambling the old streets with its pubs and traditional market, I feel the warmth that is felt when reuniting with an old friend. I've missed it in all its immovable glory – the teenage girls with pushchairs and distrait boyfriends, no longer prurient but contemplative and miserable. They are still here; kids with fags who play truant down alleyways at midday; the accents which reveal one dimensional existence.

Opportunities are not obtained with great ease and Gordon Brown's Britain has done little for a town like this in recent years. I return and I feel like a fraud, an infiltrator who barely belongs here, and who betrays the place, seeing the world, doing what he loves at little cost. I only come back when I need it; I take both it and its people for granted and the more I absent the place the more my ties to it fray, the less the people here understand me. It is a price to be paid for living the high life. I give my home no time, and it will give me none back.

On a lighter note, undoubtedly the best thing about Pontefract is its gym and the characters who inhabit it. I used it regularly, but am there less now, since I began training in Sheffield more. Recently the gym has had a revamp, and it is now adorned with 'state of the art' gear, leaving its members more inclined towards the place, with its greater aesthetic appeal. It may be a case of style over substance; few athletes ever use the pretty machines when lifting weights, but rather use old fashioned free weights.

I have in my mind a growing catalogue of functional exercises that are beneficial, especially for squash, and used sensibly could be applied to many sports. The staggering and often hilarious result of frequenting Pontefract's gym is that, despite having the option of counsel from an 'approved' physical trainer, which would be a major improvement to their own programmes, the muscle men in the gym – ill informed – carry out many of their exercises so badly that the continuous repetition will put their bodies in serious danger of injury, without them knowing it.

The two exercises that are the most commonly used by the gym monsters are the arm curl and the bench press. Now, neither exercise is of much use to any sportsmen, save perhaps for boxers and rugby players, but even then there is little reason to use them. Completely non-functional, these exercises will do one thing only, which is to make the muscle look bigger. Its impact on sporting performance, especially in a sport such as squash, is minimal.

Who cares much about sporting performance at Pontefract? Not the muscle men; their sole objective is to increase the size of their upper body. To be fair to the place, and I am alluding only to a minority of people in any one gym, muscle men can be found anywhere.

When I watch the arm curl in action, so much weight is put on the bar that the men are unable to lift it with their arms, and so their only option, God forbid they lessen the weight, is to involve the back in the exercise, which defeats the purpose.

As I lie on the floor going through my pilates and yoga exercises, I look on appalled at the dangers of over-lifting. Even funnier are the conversations I hear, in which the men sound very focused and committed and dedicated to one thing: getting bigger.

The worst thing of all is having to listen to the one character who grunts incessantly as he completes his sets, clearly intent on showing everyone how hard it is! This sort of thing is often done in the closest possible proximity to any women in the gym at the time. It is at times like this I feel most inclined to approach such a person and offer him to accompany me on the bike or stepper for an endurance blast. Then we would see how tough he is.

There is also another type of character, seen only

occasionally, who likes to train with his shirt off. Training conditions get no worse than this. Thankfully I have access to the gym in Sheffield at the EIS, used solely by athletes who strangely display much less of this self importance and self obsession, yet are twenty times the physical specimens.

* * *

I take great pleasure in returning to Pontefract after my travels. I have had a fulfilling relationship with the town and the club, whose members have steadfastly supported me throughout my career. They've travelled extensively to watch me play, especially at tournaments in Manchester, and now that there is reliable internet coverage of the world tour, the members can all gather round the big screen in the bar to watch.

The club has always been a focal point in the town, a very working-class area. It was built in 1979, spawned from the Jonah Barrington-inspired squash boom of the Seventies. There were tough times when I was in my mid-teens and the land was threatened to be taken over by developers who had provisions in place to build a supermarket. What a thought that is now. It was at this point that Mick, then a member, stepped in to save it.

In 15 years the place has gone from being ramshackle and half derelict, walls falling apart and roofs caving in, with a meagre 200 members, to looking smart with eight new courts and a new gym. There are now close to 2,000 members. We've hosted the European Club Championships, have a Premier Squash League team, and stand as an official centre of excellence. Considering what the club gives to the sport it is justified.

A squash tradition has developed, producing countless national and international players. Lee Beachill was the world No 1 and did it all based in Pontefract. The two of us were in the top 10 in the world and world team champions at the same time. There must be something right with a system that can make that happen.

I am grateful I had the opportunities in such a grounded environment. I didn't care whether the courts were grubby at one stage. It probably helped build the spirit.

And if there was a degree course on the art of helping kids to make something of themselves, then Malc would teach it. His first chapter would be titled: 'Sunday Mornings'. That's where every young player, champion or not, who has gone through his system, began. Sunday morning coaching. Me included.

There are two sessions, 10:30 and 11:30. The kids paid £1.50 back in my day – it may have gone up by now but I wouldn't be surprised if it hasn't. There can be up to 40 kids walk through the doors on any given Sunday. From these sessions they move in to Malc's midweek slots, when the legend himself allows them. Malcolm turns up every Sunday morning for the kids, but he has been helped considerably by a team of dedicated coaches who have shown great commitment in being constantly reliable and dependable.

Two of my oldest and closest pals, Kirsty McPhee and Andrew Cross, have come through Malc's system and now have connections with England Squash and Racketball and Squash Malaysia. They were two of the coaches who over the years both attended and coached on the Sunday morning sessions. Such considerable time and effort must be a big factor in the success the club has with its young people. Real hands-on, hard work of this type, by dedicated coaches, makes things happen.

Making the midweek sessions is the next step for any young kids, and getting the nod is like receiving that first England squad tracksuit. Such moments are never forgotten. Malc demands high levels of discipline from all of his players and I was treated no differently. He knew early on that I was extremely competitive and quite volatile, and so at times he bollocked me as much, if not more than he did anyone else.

His bollockings are notorious. He taught PE at my school when I was a teenager, and one hot summer afternoon I remember sitting in chemistry and hearing his loud voice booming from the tennis courts, which must have been about a mile away. I buried my head in my books with embarrassment and the teacher, trying to conduct a class, soon became frustrated enough to close the classroom window, despite the heat, to stop the unholy noise.

Like nearly all of the players that have trained with him, I too have received the famous Malcolm Willstrop ban. Most of us have been banned in some form or other by him at some stage (though he does have a soft spot for girls; they seem to have a way of emphatically escaping inclusion on this list).

It is not really the aim of the club or Malcolm to produce great squash players. That is almost a secondary part of the process. The club caters for every standard of player, not just professionals. We just happen to get the publicity. Malcolm spends just as much time with his groups of amateur club players and children as he does with the professionals, if not more. His aim is to get kids playing, and to provide them with social interaction and enjoyment through squash. He wants to teach them to become responsible and respectful adults rather than professional squash players.

17 July 2010

Malc has rewarded me with a new scrap book. He has compiled around 15 documenting my achievements through various press cuttings and photographs, and they are invaluable. He expends much effort on them and I realise I would have no organised record of my accomplishments were he not to take the time to see to them.

On the very last page of his latest effort was my picture as a blonde two year-old, taken on the Norfolk Broads, the region of my birth. I was alone in the picture, and taking up only the bottom right of the frame. I sported denim dungarees and a cute smile: it took my breath away as only a photograph can. I was struck initially by the solitary yet happy nature of the photograph, perhaps a precursory symbol.

Flashback
31 July 2000

Arriving in Manchester I am greeted by Malc, who collects me from the airport, and our team of hungover world junior champions returning from Milan gather to say goodbye.

The last two days have been entirely unforgettable, and though I don't know it now it will prove to be one of my most intense and shared sporting experiences. Perhaps that comes from the fact that we fashioned an unthinkable win over an Egyptian team we had no right to beat; or perhaps it comes from the fact that we all got on so very well. Or maybe it was because the finals party was a sensational experience, in which Milan models danced on tables, quite some vision for a 16-year-old; or possibly even because I had to carry my room-mate Phil Barker to his bed after exultant celebrations.

Going into the event, England were seeded second but a sizeable gap stood between the Egyptians and ourselves –

despite the two nations being the best in the world. Karim Darwish had blitzed the field to win the individual event, looking untouchable at No 1 string and Daryl Selby had been beaten by the opposing No 3 player, 3-0, the week before. Phil had the biggest chance, but come the day of the expected final, was blistered and jaded from brutal matches against Canada and Pakistan. We were clear underdogs.

Nobody in that cramped Milan squash club would have had us as winners, but supported by the knowledge of our ability to be gutsy and determined we had hope and belief. If anything this was one department in which we could take on the talented Egyptians.

Selby won 3-1, brilliantly, in a typically lion-hearted performance. As I warmed up on courts 100 yards away, listening to the shouts and cheers, I found myself running faster, warming up harder, so much so that I had to calm myself down.

I suddenly felt inspired and sharp. What a position to be in: young, fit and with absolutely nothing to lose against Karim Darwish, the champion. No one expected much from me, but an hour later I found myself 2-1 and match ball up after an eventful match in which I developed a mystery bladder problem that bizarrely induced a constant feeling of needing to go to the toilet. In between games, David, instead of giving me advice, was running the tap in the bathroom and making 'ssshhhh' sounds to help me. I don't know what this strange sensation was, and I have never had it since.

Someone told me later that my team-mate, Alister Walker, had even been praying in the other lavatories, such was the intensity of the situation.

I lost the match to Darwish and balled my eyes out in a broom cupboard. I remember clinging to Annette Pilling, our team manager who is three feet smaller than myself, and even Wendy Danzey, an international referee, came to my aid.

Perhaps there was something significant in the fact that I was so emotional that day. The most important woman in my life was lying in a Leeds hospital dying. Looking back, it was an outpouring of emotion that spoke of more than the mere loss of a squash match.

Sitting down in front of the court to watch Phil Barker play the deciding rubber, I could only think of having had a match ball to win the title for this team, to which I had become so close during those weeks. I had never seen or experienced anything like it before in my young life. As I sat watching Phil battle, I wasn't really aware that I was about to enter in to some of my darkest days.

Phil went 2-0 down and it appeared there was no chance. We sat dejected. Phil, though, had other ideas. He fought with incredible guts and started to pull back the deficit in the third, and won it. There was now more than a glimmer of hope; the Egyptian boy was on the back foot. After Phil won the fourth, there was only one way it could go, had to go, and anything to the contrary would have caused near insanity for all involved in England's camp. I for one would have been searching for the nearest cliff.

Then came the most incredible 90 seconds in between the fourth and fifth games. Everyone in the team and staff surrounded Phil's chair in an unprecedented series of events fuelled by great tension. Normally a coach would not accept this, but such was the intensity of the experience that both coach and manager would have been too involved to even notice. Each team member gathered around, shouting encouragement, comments that weren't remotely tactical to his face. It was accepted as the only possible reaction at such an important time. As we walked back to our seats, Abbas Kaoud, the Egyptian manager was slapping the Egyptian No 2 on the face.

On the winning point, all that was left to do was to run onto court. I don't consider myself to be a person who reacts like this very often, but this was a unique and unprecedented moment. An impartial observer could well have looked upon our raucous behaviour with disdain, but in that moment there was little chance of it being contained in any way.

In the balmy Manchester air, I head with Malc to the car, leaving behind me the three weeks of fun and happiness. I have come of age a little and Malc expresses his disgust at the fact I am wearing beads.

'What the hell have you got around your neck?'.

'Oh beads, Phil bought me them.'

'Pathetic', was Malc's response. His comment made me feel like a girl but I didn't care.

I knew Mum had gone into hospital just after I had left for Milan, but she had been in reasonable shape, still fighting her way through chemotherapy. I had been told very little about her condition over the three weeks.

We get to the car and I am full of the joys of youth and success. After a while Malc tells me we need to go to hospital immediately, without giving too much away that may cause stress during one of my finest hours.

'Oh, is she OK?'

'Well she has been in hospital since you left, and has certainly not been well enough to come out, but she's OK. Joan is with her all the time. She would really like to see you and so I think we should go immediately.'

Taken a little by surprise, I stutter: 'Absolutely'.

It is immediately apparent why I need to be there. I open the door of her private room at the Roundhay Park Hospital and our eyes meet instantly. My poor mother stirs from her vague sleep with such hope and anticipation, which tells me that she had been waiting for this moment all week. To gaze into somebody's eyes and to be completely clear that they would do absolutely anything in the world for you is something I had barely considered before, but in this very precious moment, with her ravaged by cancer, it is given immense substance.

The moment is a defining one, which will both haunt and comfort in equal measure until my dying days. It shows me the love of my mother in a guise I have never seen before. It also shows me that she is dreadfully ill, and her increased pleasure at the sight of her youngest son tells me that she is facing death. At 16 though, this eventuality is nearly impossible to process.

I'm reduced to tears. We say nothing to each other, but I move around the bed, and fall into her arms much in the way that I did all those months ago when she learnt of the first diagnosis. We both cry together for minutes, releasing so much pent up love and emotion. How special and precious these moments are I cannot begin to say. I tell her I love her, over and over again. Not for the first time, I am so glad I can at the very least give her those words to cling to. There might be little else left.

19 July 2010

I woke in the middle of the night with stomach cramps. At this moment I was struck just how deplorable debilitating or terminal illness must be. How do folks endure constant stints of chemotherapy? How awful must that be? Not only does the patient endure terrible pain but they deal with the prospect of such a thing for days and weeks beforehand. After all is said and done, a positive result may not prevail. My mum endured all this for 18 months, and still found time to go out running! So I should settle with having a night of stomach cramps without phoning the doctor.

Nevertheless, I couldn't do much but lie on the couch. I phoned England Squash to say I wouldn't make the squad sessions that were booked in for the next few days, and settled myself down in front of the TV. I watched the Brian Clough film *The Damned United*, reporting the famed football manager's explosive tenures at Derby and Leeds, and a more peaceful and outrageously successful time with Nottingham Forest. I phoned Dad and told him they are similar characters; both stubborn, opinionated, loudmouthed buggers. We laughed together, as he too had watched both the film and ITV documentary.

22 July 2010

Started to ease back in today and headed over to Sheffield to see Mark, who broke me in with some moderate strength work. Hopefully that is the end of the bug. An athlete can survive after a mere three days off; little ground is lost and the enforced rest can be a good thing.

Many sportsmen and women are unable to judge the right time to begin training after illness or injury; that obsessive compulsive streak tends to kick in and gives such driven characters a feeling that they have to train, so that they may feel the high of the workout. Erring on the side of caution all of the time never changed the world; wrapping yourself up in cotton wool is hardly conducive to getting things done, and in the case of the athlete there will often be times when the body is stiff or hampered by niggly injuries, or when illness looms.

On countless occasions over the years I have faced dilemmas and had to make decisions on whether or not to play or train through injuries and illnesses. I find watching rugby helps: the players play on, even having had 10 stitches, or with blood gushing from their heads, thinking nothing of it. I remember Tony Smith, the Warrington Rugby League coach, saying how there were times when his players played important games carrying injuries.

Squash players may not take the hits that rugby players do but because of the individual nature of the sport, there is no room for the slightest weakness at any stage.

The strangest example of this happened to me at the British Open in 2008 in Liverpool. I arrived at the tournament from Amsterdam, where England retained their European Team title, tired from a hard season and I developed a nasty chest infection before the first round. I was in a strange frame of mind, maybe lacking in freshness, and my head was all over the place. Turning up to the club for a practice hit before my match, I wondered when – not if – I would be pulling out. I was glugging cough medicine and loaded myself with paracetamol, just to make it through a light practice. I blundered through it pathetically, and was petulantly beginning to resent the fact that a bad infection decided to hit me now, at this tournament of all tournaments. I had steamrollered through the last three months, winning everything in sight, and turned up in Liverpool in an appalling mental state. If only I had given myself some breathing space a little earlier in the year.

I stood at 1-1 in the first round match with rising Pakistani player Aamir Atlas Khan, wanting to be anywhere else but on the old courts at the Liverpool cricket club. I had decided to play but for what reason I was unsure: run down, with headaches, and coughing my guts up in between games, I went over to Vanessa and just stood, almost asking her for an answer. I was doing and saying all sorts of bizarre things. Even if I had been fit enough to win the match, I knew I wouldn't be fit enough to beat the world's best players in the biggest tournament of the year, so I couldn't see the point.

'Just play James. Don't complicate things. Everything is fine. The situation is what it is. Try and relax and play. Unclutter your mind and focus on the basic things,' David said to me in between games. He worked me through one of his most difficult assignments. Tactical talk didn't even come in to it. What he had to deal with was my mindset. I was in a mess, but remained in tact so that I could win the match 3-1. I had started to relax a little, to not care.

A day later and I came through in straight games against Malaysian Ong Beng Hee. I didn't feel perfect, but it was better and things were going my way.

In the quarters I was to face Peter Barker, who had played a marathon with my Pontefract team-mate Lee Beachill, and must have been feeling it physically. What is more, Ramy, my semi-final draw, had been knocked out. His own head appeared to be in more of a state than my own. All of a sudden, with the illness in the back of my mind, my body doing its best to shake it off, things were looking much more positive. What an extraordinary example of the difference 24 hours makes in sport. I had been ready to pull out just a day ago, and now a path to the final was beginning to clear, and what is more the illness seemed to be subsiding.

Add another 48 hours and the illness had more or less vanished – probably a direct consequence of the laissez-faire attitude to the squash that I had developed and the fact I had been kept busy – and I was in the final of the British Open having beaten Peter and then Thierry Lincou 3-0, playing some of my best squash of the season. Somehow I had made it to the final to play gritty Australian David Palmer. I was fresh and knew this had turned into an immense opportunity.

Flashback
British Open final, May 2008

I stand alone, minutes before the announcements, behind a curtain which separates one half of the vast Liverpool Echo

Arena from the other. On the other side is the spectacular shining glass squash court surrounded by hundreds of people, either sitting or visiting the food stands and merchandise stalls, priming themselves for action. I stand, sweating profusely after a lengthy warm-up, and think that the moment to put everything into practice is now: those horribly hard sessions on cold mornings, the times when I got off my backside and worked when no one else was watching and no one else cared; this is the time that work comes into play.

I remember watching this tournament at Wembley as a young kid. The Khans, Jahangir and Jansher, Rodney Martin, Chris Dittmar and Peter Marshall going at it in front of 2,000 people. Isn't it strange how things change and move on so quickly? It silently and simultaneously appalls and pleases me that I am now them.

After a dreadful day, spent feeling sick with nerves, it is now time to play in the British Open final. The fact that I was on the verge of pulling out is now not even a thought. I have a quick word with my brother David, who won the over-35 championship earlier. I watched it, and think to myself what a wonderful tribute it would be to Mum if we could do the double.

I complete the last bits of a routine I depend on. I glance away and see David Palmer, my illustrious opponent, in the opposite corner of the oversized area. There is a grand entrance, and the adrenalin sets in. I say positive thoughts to myself.

After the knock up I sit in my chair and listen to Malc's last comments. Sweat drips off my face and head and my hand shakes slightly as I open my bag to reach for a wristband. I had packed all my drinks in the same compartment as my shirts, headbands and wristbands. One has leaked onto my clothes.

The wristbands and bandannas are all soaked. What is

the point of being so obsessive compulsive and not getting the packing of your bag right before a match like this?

Stressed and angry, I look at Vanessa in the crowd and ask her if she could get me some wristbands. I had been struggling with sweating all week on that court, and I needed them. I had already been through the implausible situation where Malc had to cut my hair in between games in the match with Barker because the floor was so slippy. It was one of the only things I could think of that could help. Malc's hairdressing skills left a lot to be desired and when I look at the photographs from the time I can't help but be reminded of Friar Tuck.

Nevertheless, I am nowhere in the first game, merely a rabbit in the headlights. I settle myself before the second and play more assuredly and the combat is more level, but I lose it. So I'm two down before I know it and the dream is falling through my fingers; a ghastly feeling. Everything is happening so quickly, and I seem to be able to do nothing. This was not what I had expected. I am the man in form here, not him. I won five in a row in March, my best spell ever, and he has had a dodgy run coming in to this. I have to do something quickly.

I sip a sports drink out of necessity. I listen but do not speak to Malc. He gets it spot on. 'It's OK, the second was vastly improved. The game is still alive, concentrate on the starts here. This is not over.' There are one or two tactical reinforcements, but they are minor.

I gain the advantage in the third, quite resoundingly, but the margin is fine. By doing this I give myself a monumental lift, because I now have momentum despite the deficit.

As the ferocity of the competition cranks up a notch in the fourth – fast, long rallies – there are more breaks and the court needs to be wiped increasingly. Gaining the ascendancy in the fourth, I feel roused the more we play. I can sense Palmer's frustrations creeping in; an odd muttering, an argument with the ref, and my squash is too good in the fourth, but not by much. It is tantalisingly close.

Sitting in the chair before the fifth I listen to Malc, nodding and saying 'yes' forcefully to every word. There's not a lot he can do tactically at this stage but reinforce, so desperate and intense is the situation, but his tone of voice and reassurance are important. I glance over to the people in my corner. Everyone I love is sitting there, wanting it for me, and for themselves. It occurs to me at that moment that earlier in the day David came back from two down to win the over-35 title and I might be on the verge of repeating it, making the fairytale even sweeter.

In the fifth I stand in the right service box at 9-6 up, the finish line now perilously close. I am two points from becoming the British Open Champion, from being the *inspiration*, not the inspired.

A monumental rally ensues and Palmer stays in it with great determination. I am only slightly stretched in the front right as my forehand drop shot hits the top of the tin, and it proves to be costly. It is certainly an unforced error, despite my feeling so tired. The outcome of a British Open final can hinge on a shot like this. Had it gone up, I doubt he would have retrieved the ball, and the title was all but won. What follows is the most bizarre and unsatisfying end to a squash match I can remember. It happens on this day, of all days.

Palmer gets back to 9-9, one of those points I gift to him by mis-hitting a ball into the floor, inexplicably, from the back right. I could hit that shot a million times and would probably never fail, but tonight the Pontefract club league player in me makes an unwelcome appearance to produce a dud of a shot. It is mystifying how I can manage to mess up a shot so convincingly after all the time I have spent on court over the years. Peter Nicol said in his commentary that it was concentration. He was wrong. It was a freak shot.

But I compose myself and win a stroke, which could have gone either way, to take me to match point. At 10-9, serving to win the British Open, I serve at his body. He sprays the return down the middle of the court. My racket goes back. I can't swing. My heart pumps and I wait for the words 'stroke to Willstrop'. I ask the question to the referee, my arms half aloft, ready to celebrate. The referee calls a let.

Disbelief. I don't like to blame referees but it is a stroke. My head is in my hands. At least two of the referees called it a let. But how? There was no room to play the shot with David so close. I am now faced with two options: come off court, enraged, and complain about this utter balls-up. Or stay composed – as I have been taught and as is my way – and carry on with the match ball I still hold. I choose the latter. I walk to the service box *knowing* I should be British Open Champion. How can this happen?

Incensed inside, but calm out, I serve again. Another stupendous rally, and a stroke allows him to get back to 10 apiece. But I respond brilliantly, working him out of position, to win the next rally and give myself another bite of the cherry.

He hits a good cross-court that unfortunately lands in the nick. It's followed up with yet another sapping rally, one which sees me out of position and sprinting as he drops the ball to the front left. He breaks his racket but he now stands with a match ball. He then wants a stroke but doesn't get one.

It is tantalising. I can hardly control my body. I try to breathe, but struggle not to think of winning this match, and shake instead. I try to think of each rally, to play my best shots, to do what I know and have practised all these years.

Then comes the final blow: after some cat and mouse

rallying on his match ball, after 111 minutes, I take him into the front right with a decent enough shot. Surely he shouldn't be able to apply much pressure with his return? His reply is a mis-hit that fumbles its way just above the tin in the front left. I have no chance. I amble to the front of the court, unable to comprehend how I now stand here the loser. Distraught, I hold myself together, shaking his hand, before walking off.

It won't come as a surprise that I replay the mis-hits and the forehand drop error in the fifth game countless times over the course of the night, but the frequency of these flashbacks is outnumbered by piercing thoughts of the match ball stroke. To have effectively won the match destroys me for days and months afterwards. I can cope with the mis-hits – they are Palmer's doing – far more than the stroke decision.

28 July 2010. National Training Camp, Manchester.

Getting through some hard sessions.

Anyone can train for hours averagely, but not everyone can train for minutes really well.

I'm approaching each workout with this in mind: trying to train with quality and not worrying about quantity. I often take consolation in the fact that all the toughest training sessions, however hard, are relatively short in the whole scheme of things. If the session in question is one of the killer kind, a gut-wrencher, isn't it gratifying to know that in a short time, maybe an hour or two, the pain will subside and you may sleep, eat, or relax?

It was a welcome move to mix things up in the afternoon, and a video analysis session fitted in perfectly. William Forbes, the lead performance analyst for squash, videos the player from all angles on the court, slowing down or speeding up the movement, whereupon the coaches (and player) can analyse and make corrections or recommend changes. The session is purely technical and it often throws up something of interest.

The afternoon was broken up quite nicely with some solo practice, ghosting and strength work. We headed back to eat and then I collapsed in to bed. The England team have practically lived at the Holiday Inn in Manchester this summer.

29 July 2010

Had a hit at Pontefract and felt tired and lethargic. It had to be a steady session, after the squad onslaught and with an annual eight man tournament in Cleethorpes ahead. The event is perfectly placed as a warm-up to the Aussie Open and providing I can survive it – the tournament necessitates three matches in 24 hours, on a boiling hot court with a high tin – it could be a great sharpener.

The following days will be all elbow grease: a long trip to the Far East lies ahead and it promises to be one of the most challenging spells of travel that I have ever undertaken. I find sitting on planes laborious in the extreme, but the thought of playing matches at the end of it excites me immeasurably. I really do feel cheered to be off again and I can't imagine myself tiring of this life one bit, as the years saunter by. First stop, the Australian Open in Canberra.

FIVE

BACK TO THE GRIND

11 August 2010

Australian Open, Canberra. Here we go again, I've been up since 5:45 this morning. Took a pill but this time it wouldn't send me off, a disconcerting thought as there is no way I can't be tired. If the pills stop working I really am in trouble. I find myself at the breakfast room as soon as it opens at 6:30. Other players have started to do the same, which is a relief.

Since arriving in Australia all I have done is battle to sleep, waking up between 4 and 6am every morning, and my reliance on sleeping pills is becoming alarming. It is distressing and draining and leaves me in a foul mood.

When I sleep badly I am reminded how important and rewarding it is to sleep well. When in a more normal pattern, free of the difficulties of changing time zones, it is not something we tend to think of; usually we sleep and get on with the day, not realising quite how important the sleep part is. Right now I have great sympathy with people who continuously struggle with insomnia, and understand their frustrations.

As a sportsman, not sleeping has greater consequences. To get through a working day without training and playing high level sport is one thing, but to expect to compete at your highest physical potential on the back of no rest is not feasible.

After my hit today I was offered a lift home from the club by a jovial chap with a thick Aussie accent. The type who pronounced my name 'Jymes' not 'James', and 'yeyah' not 'yeah'.

His name was Richard, a member of the club, and he had seemed keen to meet me. I presumed that he would want to hear everything there is to know about squash but to the contrary, the dialogue was centred around the political structures or places of interest in Canberra. He proceeded, without asking, to give me a tour of the city, hardly stopping for breath during a tirade which covered much of the history of Australian politics. He also took great care to explain all the locations of different countries' embassies within Canberra. In fact, the embassies seemed to be quite an obsession of his and I was his outlet; he acted like a budding tour guide, with only one thing on his mind.

'I bit nawun has shawn ya anythin of the cidy have thay? Aah mean, there's so mach to fakun see it's a shyme ya have to be insoide the howtel every day.'

'Yes, well, we tend to concentrate on playing, eating and sleeping. Not much time for anything else.' I did just want to go back to the hotel, and Canberra hadn't struck me as a city created with the sightseeing industry in mind.

The embassy infatuation began. 'Awl the myjor embassies are lowcated in this area. Here, look, South Africa, Islamic, French. Chinese awver there look. They're awl owver this area. And, here, look ere, that's the Priyme Minister's house.'

'And who is that at the moment?' I said. One of very few questions I was given the chance to ask. 'Julia Gillard. I'm a liberal miself. There ya go look, British Embassy. Any problems you have now here in Austrylia, and that's ya plyce. Bang. Ya go there. If ya lose ya passport: bang. That's where you're at. Yeyah.'

Slight pause. I changed the subject. 'Are you married?'

'Aah no, but I was once! The wife, she had issues. And here, here are the Aboriginals camping out feeling sorry faw themselves.' It hadn't taken him long to get back to the history of Australia. 'But naah, I'm much happier now. I got me a rottwheeler. She's a good thing. Never gives me any grief, like the wiyfe did. She was a nutter in the end. All hassle and nag with the wife. I'm happy with the rottwheeler.'

I can't argue with that.

12 August 2010

The build-up to my match with local favourite David Palmer has been intense. Someone mentioned that it could be his last Aussie Open, even his last year, so he was geared up to perform here. I was pleased to beat him in four concentrated games.

The two of us haven't played for a while, but our recent matches have gone his way, a few of them in England, so it was particularly sweet to beat him comfortably in his home territory. It was a big result so early in the season, and good to be back in the swing of things with a win over a top 10 player.

A few people had been quick to criticise me for my strategy against him with regard to those losses. The losing streak to him was building at one stage and I had heard all the usual speculation from all sorts of directions: some thought I had a 'mental block' (people love that phrase), some thought that vegetarianism was stopping me from crossing the winning line. It never ceases to amaze me how bluntly people can talk, as if for all the world they might know what they are talking about.

I even heard people speak critically of Palmer, implying that I should have been beating him because his movement was diminishing as he got older. These people should have tried playing him, one of the sport's greatest athletes. I certainly didn't see much of a drop in his movement in the last matches we had, or even today, just the same brilliant athlete I had always known. His commitment and ability to perform on big occasions is legendary.

People have started to write off Thierry Lincou, like Palmer, not for any other reason than they are getting older and therefore are expected to decline; many have written off Amr Shabana before. It is a most easy thing to do as players pass the thirty mark, yet it can often be an inopportune assumption. After all, they are world No 1's and world champions.

13 August 2010

I'm up at 3am again, and can't get back off. Infuriated, I go to reception to ask for another room so that I don't disturb Saurav, which proves to be too much hard work for the night porter who gives me rehearsed phrases about the computer system not being able to get the rate for the tournament, and that I will have to pay the full rate. I look at him in a state of exasperation, tearing my hair from my head, claiming that the year is 2010, and that things are surely more simply dealt with when just pen and paper are involved.

However, I settle for the situation and down more pills, finally managing to sleep until 10:30 and get the requisite number of hours to enable me to function reasonably on a squash court. The sleep deficit doesn't seem to be affecting the quality of my squash. I am playing well and deal with Shabana in clinical fashion.

14 August 2010

Standing around by the back of the court, sweating during the warm-up before my semi-final against Nick, I consider, and am duly convinced that the worst part about playing competitive squash is this part right now, the waiting; worse than the travelling, and worse than the hard sessions.

I watch the women's match between England's Alison Waters and Rachael Grinham, during which I try to coordinate and time the warm-up to coincide with the end. Today there is a startling sense of déjà vu; it always seems to be Rachael I'm waiting for. I try to remember the times where the Australian's matches have preceded my own, of which there have been many.

Without being disrespectful, Rachael isn't the easiest player to anticipate (perhaps one of the reasons she is so hard to play) and it seems to be a common theme. Her matches have an uncanny knack of making warm-ups impossible. I have seen her lose games easily, win games easily, and come back from the dead just as I thought she had no chance. I must tell her how often it seems to be happening.

Now, she is in the process of chasing down Alison's 2-0 lead, and as I peer in through the curtain which cordons off the players area, the score stands at 8-8 in the fourth: we could be on in four minutes, or twenty four minutes. If Rachael wins this game I will be into my fourth warm-up of the night. It was in Hong Kong last year, I think, where she lost to her sister 3-0 in about 20 minutes, that I barely had any time to warm-up, so quickly was the match over, and so quickly were we asked to follow on afterwards.

It goes to five games.

The worst bit is the waiting, the nerves. Once on court, it is time to relax and play, and to not think. The final preparations done, it is time to let go. Nick and I lock horns once more.

Sixty minutes of sheer intensity follows; an onslaught of pace that is very difficult to cope with. I can't say that I am in my worst shape, yet I am nowhere near him on this day. His physical capacity is too much. I feel good on there in spells, and feel like I can control certain phases from the middle, but his nagging tendency to relentlessly fetch each ball and hit it back with added interest requires that I play several more shots than I do against anybody else to win a rally. It explains why he is the world's best.

I am on a long losing streak with him, so the people like to say; his age and strength count for him when we play no doubt. I am happy with what I am doing and hopefully in time can gain some ground physically. There is a lot to learn, and many improvements to make, but the challenge of matching someone at the peak of his powers in sporting terms is ultimately enticing and requires skill and determination to overcome.

Back at the hotel I need to let go and give my mind a rest after the mental and physical exertions of the week. There is no question which DVD I shall watch: the film *Wilde*, a biopic of the king of the paradoxical quip, who made the banality and conformity of Victorian society humorous. His life story is perhaps as tragic as it gets. Yet again, the film raises my dwindling spirit, allowing me to forget the disappointment, and it sends me off into the night, in which I sleep soundly for the first time since leaving England. Tomorrow there is no match for which to prepare. Sod's law is the apt phrase I believe.

21 August 2010

It's 10 years to the day Mum died and she has been on my mind. The memories of that period are always prominent throughout August. The isolation is crushing and it's not fair to expect anyone to understand or to feel the same way at the same time, about the same person, however much they try to sympathise. Grief, by definition, is bound to be intensely personal. Even the people who knew and loved my mum to the same degree, her twin Joan, my dad or even my brothers, seem naturally inclined to stay closed up about it, and we seem unable to reach out to each other. Instead, we grieve, year after year, alone.

This time of year especially recalls the stench in the hospital corridor, the pained expressions so visible on the faces of each patient on that dreary ward in which Mum spent her final days. That period, those last days and weeks, were full of grief and sorrow, yet every time I stepped out of the hospital after a visit, I remained surprised to see the world still turning as usual. Exposure to the realities of illness and death on a daily basis made me feel as if I'd been woken up from a dream that left me longing to go back to sleep. They say ignorance is bliss and I've never been more convinced of that than during those final days. Time seemed to stand still for a while and I couldn't imagine reverting back to my carefree life of squash and petty problems. I felt like I had been given a glimpse on the inside, of an environment in which doctors and nurses are immersed daily. Mum worked as a theatre nurse and it seemed obvious in retrospect that she knew what was coming well before those close to her did.

Every August it all becomes vivid once again and the world seems a little darker. The grief does get easier over time, but it never ever goes away.

23 August 2010

The Hong Kong climate is a complete contrast to that of Australia: it is stiflingly humid, which is no problem indoors because of the air conditioning, and we arrive in a positive frame of mind, happy to be back in these sticky climes, a city now entirely familiar to all the players. I arrived early on Saturday morning for the Hong Kong Open, heading straight for the breakfast buffet.

A passenger bus in Manila has been hijacked; there were many Chinese on board, making their way back to Hong Kong from holiday. Four people have been killed. The hijacker, a former police constable, had lost his job and decided to take it all out on random people minding their own business in a bus.

28 August 2010

Replaying the match is stopping me from sleeping. I lost 3-0 to Ramy Ashour in the quarter-final. Everything felt alien and too much like hard work: difficult to swallow when I have been thinking I am in good shape. I lost the last two matches against him in demoralising fashion, and I can't help but question myself after such a good summer's work. By not stepping up to the plate I have left myself deflated.

I came off court and had the most enormous strop, throwing bags and rackets around and reacting badly towards a child who was in my path and had innocently asked for an autograph. When I lose perspective in the immediate aftermath of a bad match I don't like myself. I sit here in the middle of the night thinking how immaturely I behaved. It probably wasn't all that bad. Although, now I can see that nothing is achieved by it.

I can't bear losing in such an average manner, no matter at whose hands. I love coming to Hong Kong and I love to travel the world playing squash, but if in the end it makes you miserable then why go through with it? After the summer's work, which has been mentally tough, and as hard this year as ever, to put in such a mediocre performance makes me feel like giving up. I feel negative,

1. 'Success! Winning the Tournament of Champions, Grand Central, New York, January 2010. My finest hour on a squash court marks the beginning of my diaries.' © Rob White

2. 'Sowing the seeds in the gym with Mark Campbell.'

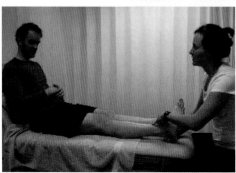

3. 'Ali Rose has her work cut out in between tournaments.'

4. 'Jade Elias treats a heavy dead leg, courtesy of Gaultier's knee, in the semis of the British Grand Prix.' © 2011 Fritz Borchert / Squashinternational.com

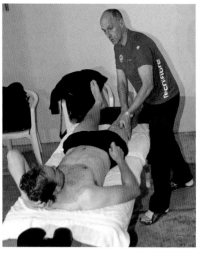

5. 'Phil Newton has been holding the bodies of English squash players together for years. Here he treats me after the World Open semi final in 2010.' © 2011 Fritz Borchert / Squashinternational.com

6. 'It won't bend! My body gives way after nearly two hours of brutality'. © Steve Line/Squashpics.com

7. 'Sylvan and Caroline Glain can do little about the cramp at the Canary Wharf Classic in March'. © Steve Line/Squashpics.com

8. 'Someone was smiling on my two brothers and I when they handed out mums. Lesley in a happy moment during her illness'.

9. 'Malc and Mick pose with me after a win at the 2010 World Open in
Saudi Arabia'. © 2011 Fritz Borchert/Squashinternational.com

10. 'Lucky man. Sharing a laugh with Vanessa after a win in 2007.'
© 2011 Fritz Borchert/Squashinternational.com

11. 'The terrain makes it 'even more of a challenge for my oversized limbs'. Damon and I attack the hills.'

12. 'In dire pain whilst pushing up the Colorado trails. Vanessa and Terry in the background.'

13. 'Having a post-run ice bath in the freezing river in Estes Park, Colorado, with Damon.'

14. 'Malcolm sometimes finds himself doing anything but talking in between games. Here he cools me down before the fifth game of the British Open Final in 2008.' © Steve Line/Squashpics.com

15. 'Embroiled in battle with David Palmer during the same final.'
© Steve Line/Squashpics.com

16. 'Not happy with the floor, I discuss the playing conditions in Delhi with tournament director Andrew Shelley.'
© Steve Line/Squashpics.com

17. 'After two hours I get the better of David Palmer at the Commonwealth Games in Delhi, to the delight of the front row.'
© Steve Line/ Squashpics.com

18. 'After a severe 24 hours, I succumb to Ramy Ashour in five at the 2010 Kuwait Open.' © Steve Line/Squashpics.com

19. 'Locked in combat with Nick during the early throes of the World Open Final, 2010.' © Steve Cubbins/Squashsite.co.uk

20. 'The two men who have given selflessly to my career.
Malcolm asks for more while David looks on.'
© David Barry

and that I am not near Nick and Ramy after these tournaments.

However bad I am feeling, Nick will probably feel worse, after his match in the quarters. He went down to our England team-mate Peter Barker for the first time, and he lost his composure, throwing his racket at the glass wall and ending the match angrily. The crowd jeered in response, and he reacted by saying that he was injured.

Peter and I have endured loss after loss against him recently, so he deserves some credit for one of his finest wins, a reward for all the hard work and dedication. Ramy will now overtake Nick as world No 1.

30 August 2010

Two utterly blissful days spent alone in the house, doing whatever I want. The washing can wait. I cooked food, and read. Two sensational sleeps and I'm ready to go again.

As I parked my car at Pontefract I saw Kath Smith, the resident dance instructor at the club, who I have known for years. We passed each other at the entrance; I smiled at her and she looked back at me, but made no expression whatever, almost looking straight through me. Did she not even recognise me? Have I been away for that long?

Indeed, I am now away from home that much that I often return to see that children I know have become young adults, but is it now so out of hand that I am not recognised by the people I have known all my life?

2 September 2010

Malc reminded me about a forthcoming exhibition at Lockwood Park club in Huddersfield tomorrow night. He then began to talk about me 'having songs ready'.

Several years ago Malc and I struck up a friendship with Sylvan, the high-class massage therapist whose first profession I have already mentioned was in music. He was a music producer at the time. Sylvan became a good friend and Malcolm came up with the idea of creating a band of musicians and squash players, with interests in music.

I had always sung, Lee Beachill played guitar, and England team strategist Stafford Murray was in his own band. We came together every now and again as *Lost for Words* and played on the night of exhibition matches, mixing the two. Malcolm figured that squash might not be enough for some people, so if he could offer them a band in the bar afterwards it would add significantly to the evening's entertainment, drawing more punters in.

The nights provided good entertainment and they were at times very enjoyable, but they were hard work, especially for Sylvan and the professional musicians who would have to transport equipment around and travel quite long distances for little money. It became impractical, and doing the squash and then attempting to sing songs afterwards, often on the back of little rehearsal time, became stressful. Malcolm sat and watched, admiring his creation, perhaps not aware of the toll it took on those who had to perform. For these reasons the band has done less and less in recent times.

Performing in front of crowds is wonderful, but it is something many find incredibly difficult. I really have enjoyed doing exhibition evenings but there are times when I would rather be anywhere else. People who entertain are often envied by the public. It appears to be a charmed life, so glamorous, with so much admiration coming your way but there is more to it than that.

After the conversation I had with Malc today it seems the band may be finished, although he has threatened this before. In reply to his 'songs' request on the phone, after telling me that one of the other singers had let him down, I said I knew nothing about the band   playing in Huddersfield, and that I hadn't had time to think about singing anyway. As far as I was concerned it was squash only as this was what he had told me. I had squads and training coming out of my ears, and I couldn't take on being Mick Jagger too. He then burst into a venomous rant towards anyone he could think of. He had promised the club the band and suddenly found he had no one to sing. He flew off the handle, telling me again that he had had enough of trying to organise these nights which none of 'you' seem to enjoy. I told him 'yes', I think it would be a good idea to stop them. He put the phone down on me.

As it was, the exhibition was difficult. The courts were slippery, Malc and I weren't getting on – I was admittedly being petulant – and the squash was conducted with five players involved rather than two. It made the whole thing disjointed and amateurish in my opinion. The band just about got through it.

The members at the club seemed to have a great time, and it was important that despite all our differences, we produced what the club thought was a good night. The club members and organisers are good people and deserved a big night to mark the opening of the new courts there.

FLASHBACK
2003

One day at home, in the house I had once shared with Mum, sitting as I sometimes did, gazing at her pictures during a quiet moment of the day, I remember sobbing myself dry.

In the aftermath of this one episode, I turned on the

television and skipped music channels, when onto the screen came a bequiffed figure wearing a white blazer, waving his microphone cord and arms in a way that was awkward, yet compelling. I didn't recognise the song but I was immediately struck by how clear his diction was and found myself surprised that I could hear every word he said.

'*Irish Blood, English Heart, this I'm made of. There is no-one on earth I'm afraid of*', he practically snarled. It was powerful, angry yet melodic, and I was immediately drawn to it. '*No regime can buy or sell me.*' With those words I was transfixed, and unbeknown to me at the time, the bloke with the white blazer was going to inspire me in ways I could never have imagined. I bought his new album. Apparently he was on a comeback. I played the first song and he told me through swooning vocals, '*America: your head's too big. America, your belly is too big.*'

It may not have been the most literate statement of his career, but I found it hilarious and appreciated such honesty. I had never heard music like it, and it was a world away from the insipid garbage that is all over the radio waves. The man's music was saying something, through unusual phrases and words, in the sweetest, slow burning way. He called himself Morrissey.

This is where an infatuation with words really began and my introduction to Morrissey undoubtedly rekindled an interest in the writers I had studied at school, who in turn provided comfort through their work during the sad times. My dad says that I always look for the words in music. If he doesn't like something that I am listening to, he'll say: 'I take it this is about the words'.

Morrissey came along at a good time. This weird sounding man became a helpful diversion. From then on, during those empty moments within days, spent in cars, on trains, in that house, I put Morrissey on. And how strange it felt that someone I didn't know could communicate with me through a song better than some of my friends and family. In the midst of our loss I was neither there for them nor they for me. There was seldom any talking to each other about it, except fleetingly and superficially.

14 September 2010

Meanwhile, training continues apace and, having studied the videos from Hong Kong and Australia, I have designed a one-off ghosting session which almost replicates the intervals during the matches with Nick and Ramy. It was interesting to find that the gaps in between rallies are much shorter than I thought.

The length of rallies with Ramy were generally much shorter than those I played against Nick, and the recovery time was also shorter, as Ramy likes to serve quickly. It probably didn't need a rocket scientist to work that out but it was still interesting to look at the stats.

The day, however, almost went tits up when no sooner had I got on court with Malc, I realised it was an ice rink because of works they had been doing at Pontefract. It was clear there was a film of dust that had settled. I know Malc thinks I'm complicated with floors and balls, so in view of last week's events I would rather this hadn't happened.

'Sorry. I can't play on here, but I'll go and practise alone.' No one else was complaining and this was Malc's first attempt to convince me that the courts might be okay. 'Two slipped last night, otherwise everybody said they were fine', he said.

'They said they were fine because they daren't mention it to you. Nobody ever wants to question you. Don't you realise how intimidating you are to some people? The courts are not even playable.'

15 September 2010

Won my first round at the British Grand Prix in Manchester and now have a day off. The difficult thing is judging how much work to do coming into a tournament. The idea is to keep on the boil, something that is always easier said than done, and something I still get wrong at times, even after doing it all these years.

I find sharpening work in low volumes most effective in the few days before an event and a complete day off recharges the system and gathers all the energy that I might need during the week. Having a rest day in the middle of an event can also make it slightly tricky, especially having had a relatively easy first round. Depending on the amount of work done in the week leading in, too many easy days can be detrimental. I did some fast ghosting repetitions to blow the lungs out and stay sharp. Ideally when the matches are easy it is preferable to keep going, not rest! It is later in the event that the days off are needed.

The *Daily Express* wanted to take press officer Howard Harding's offer of a 'story' and print a semi-controversial article on Nick and I in the lead up to the event. It seems the only thing that can get squash in the papers is a spat between players, but what a terrible shame they feel unable to publish genuine sporting stories. It is an indictment of these dreary publications that they are governed by gossip and hearsay, and rely in most cases on a 'story'; it is even sadder that we all read, and believe them.

The *Daily Mail*'s response to Howard was 'unless one of them is going out with Jordan or something then we can't run it'. If this is the only response they can muster regarding two of Britain's best sportsmen then they can keep their right wing chip wrap.

19 September 2010

Lying on the bed after a five game win today against Gaultier. I played for 100 minutes, not a large part of the day you would think, but the preparation before and the recovery after is long and focused and there really is nothing else of any consequence that can be done in the aftermath. My head aches from the intensity and my right calf throbs from a dead leg I received during a collision in the third. In the final tomorrow, but can hardly move. Not a good feeling.

20 September 2010

I wake up and munch on some cereals and fruit in my room. The next thing is to test the body, most notably the calf which took a beating. Greg's knee violently connected with it and I'm finding it hard to walk on the first attempt, which is worrying when a major final is a matter of hours away. I just hope that it will wear off as I begin to move around.

I get myself ready for a physio session with Jade at Sportcity. She does some steady massage on the bad area before sticking needles into the surrounding region of the calf. At the mere mention of the needles I begin to sweat profusely, but grit my teeth, swearing occasionally.

The leg begins to move more freely despite being severely restricted. The final with Ramy is decent quality but I run out of steam. I allow him to work me far too hard and I hit a wall. I win the second for only a few points, god only knows how, but the squash has to be exceptional to do so, and I know how hard it is to maintain. Yesterday was damaging and I thought I had more in the tank. I was rooted. He won the third and fourth at a canter. Cue a filthy mood.

I try to talk to people at Sportcity after the match but not very hard. I am miserable again. The sense of anti-climax is as strong as ever. I have let people down.

The ever-present threat of injury and illness looms large as the start of the Commonwealth Games nears. I sometimes think to myself that one roll of the ankle now or a pull of a muscle and the Games experience is over. Vanessa has had a cold this week, so I haven't been near her and I'm sleeping in the study.

Every time I walk on court at the moment I warm-up with more diligence, to limit the chances of getting injured. I sometimes wonder if it would be better to back off during sessions, just to save myself. Every time I get on a plane I wash my hands an extra time, or take an extra dose of nasal spray. It is a curious state of mind, always being so obsessively vigilant, and comes about because the Commonwealths only take place every four years, and if illness and injury can be avoided then they absolutely must. Ultimately I end up wasting energy. If something bad is going to happen it will probably happen; there is no way training can be done half-heartedly. Sometimes it is a matter of letting go of all the mental baggage.

FLASHBACK
4 March 2009

Rampant, I storm through the reception area of Leeds' Chapel Allerton club into the frosty air of a spring night. Instantly my body registers the palpable extremes of temperature, having gone from the warm court to this within seconds. I launch my racket at the low wall barricading the tennis courts and then pick it up again. I look around to see if anyone caught a glimpse, but in all truth I am beyond caring, and would only have repeated the act with greater ferocity had there been any such presence. I smash the racket and it is no more.

Kneeling down near to the tennis courts, I scream. I can't do this any more. I can't want it this much, and work so hard for it, only to suffer setback after setback with this bloody injury. I can't do it. I convince myself at that precise moment, within the glare of all that pent-up intensity that it is the end. I now opt for the easy life, with none of the extremes, none of the excess.

Later, I will cringe at the extent of my self-pity. I feel sorry for myself because of an ankle injury! On the floor at the edge of the car park, I ask why. I have conceded my match against Alister Walker in the Yorkshire League; every lunge I made caused stabs of pain from the bone spur that I first contracted back in August, the injury I thought had cleared. After the numerous injections, scans and treatments I have undergone during the last eight months, I am faced with the fact that it had never gone away.

I go back inside and see Vanessa looking for me. I sweep past her in a rage, and then shout something at my dad who follows. They both accompany me into a dark area by the courts. I sit there, taking my shoes and socks off in utter disgust.

I shout at them as if it is their fault. 'The same annoying pain, not going away! Since August I've rested and trained without impact, and had more rest and had more treatment. Nothing has changed, it's the same as it ever was. I'm back to square one!' They offer me ice, which I decline. I've tried ice a thousand times. It is pointless.

In order to counteract the injury, something more drastic needs to be done. I haven't trained consistently for months now, and it has shown through my mediocre achievements: I have a string of quarter-final results to my name. I had to pull out of last week's Virginia tournament with a virus. Nothing is really happening. I have been working all my life to achieve, and simply settling for being middle of the road won't cut it. I phone Alison immediately and tell her. I can hear disappointment in her voice: she has been working hard to get rid of this, and she isn't happy either. 'Come in tomorrow morning, we'll have a look. It might not be anything we can sort out without surgery'.

With these words my attitude changes ever so slightly. Surgery hadn't been mentioned before, and it gives me some hope that an operation, that last-ditch scenario, could rid me of the problem.

I wake up and see Ali. She looks at me for five minutes, prods around the ankle, hits the nasty area where the bone spur is, causing me to gasp, and the decision is made. 'We need to refer you'. Suddenly I am ecstatic. At least something might make it better now, no more stabbing in the dark.

May 2009

After the operation I had a week at home before taking a holiday in Dublin with my friends. James, Nathan and Charlie, my pals from school days, together with John, were great company that week. Vanessa was playing in the Irish Open and it was a perfect time for a holiday. I wasn't going to let the fact that I couldn't walk stop me. So off I hopped, on crutches to Dublin. I have very fond memories of a wonderful trip, where we spent time in bars and restaurants, me with the crutches. My upper body got strong!

Busy bars were tough going, but the Irish were good at saving me a stool, and John would escort me to the toilet, clearing the way, bouncer-like. It shouldn't really have worked but it did. I just had to go easy on the daily excursions, of which there were very few anyway. Instead I sat in the flat and ate chocolate. The evening alcohol eased the pain of the raw wound. All in all it was a good decision.

On my return I went straight to see Alison for my first treatment. I was hardly positive that we would make any ground, since the wound was improving but sore, and the ankle was deeply stiff and immobile.

The dressing came off, and she got to work: the treatment consisted of massage and mobility work. When I say massage, I don't mean massage in its generally considered form. It was more like torture. Alison has never let me forget an article I wrote in the *Yorkshire Evening Post* describing her sessions of treatment. In it, I concluded that they were very different and sometimes excruciatingly painful. I happened to mention that there was no oil, candles or soft music involved in Ali's sessions and instead of a green tea or a glass of water at the end of it, you are more likely to receive a sheet of paper with diagrams of prescribed rehab exercises for homework.

What happened to me that day, my first day of treatment after the op, was a good example. How I didn't die of the pain I don't know. Ali didn't subscribe to my theory that it would be too early to treat the ankle with any great venom. She pushed into it with her hands, pressing in to the foot heavily, without any hesitation.

'I take it you know what you are doing!' I screeched. 'This is disgustingly painful ...'

My teeth biting into my arm, the bed, whatever I could bite, I was demonstrative in my pleadings, to the point where I was begging her to stop. Seeing my profuse sweating, and the fighting back of tears, she said: 'I know it hurts, but we need to get it moving, and we need to eat away at the scar tissue.'

Talk about pain. It was the most intense 45 minutes I can remember. The day after this first treatment, I was so desperate to train that I rung Mark to ask him if I could go to the gym, despite my crutches and my having use of only one leg. He said we could do some upper body, and some left leg work. I was excited.

I woke up and went through my mobility exercises as usual. In the mornings it was difficult, but if I kept moving it got better. That particular morning I could not believe how much the ankle had improved. It was miles better in fact! My God, this was brilliant. I almost didn't need the crutch! Was Ali a witch? Is she really that good?

I got to the gym and during the session I left my crutch in the corner, hopping everywhere I needed to. Mark laughed at the limits we faced, but we did everything we could which did not involve my right leg. It was fairly surreal as far as training sessions go, but by the end of it, to my amazement, with the blood pumping, I had started to realise I didn't need the crutch and what's more I barely needed to hop. Such was my improvement that I could actually walk. I had been transformed within 24 hours. It was a revelation, after two weeks of incapacitation.

By mere coincidence, I walked in to the reception at the EIS and saw Ali, who had come to Sheffield for meetings. She looked at me ... then looked away, probably thinking it couldn't be me ... and looked again, utterly puzzled.

'You...it's you! You are WALKING?!' she exclaimed, perplexed.

'Sorry. Was that a question or a statement?', I said with a smile forming.

'How the *hell* are you walking?'

We chatted for a minute or two in amazement at the transformation. She said she had never seen or expected such improvement in such a short period. I left her, and she still couldn't take her eyes off me. I think she was quite pleased with herself that day. The recovery was well under way. She was happy with her work and I was happy there might be an end to the run of quarter-final results.

22 September 2010

We've had to listen to the mainstream media having a field day, reporting remorselessly on the Commonwealth Games venues, which if tabloid scavengers are to be believed is uninhabitable. The newspapers are leading with the story of Delhi's deficiencies, showing pictures of a bridge leading to the main stadium that collapsed, and of athletes' living quarters covered in filth and waste, beds decorated with the odd animal footprint. There have even been reports of snakes in the village.

There is photographic evidence but somehow I can't imagine it is all as bad as they are making out. The media will not write anything positive because positive stories don't sell. Squash players should know: in the last decade or so squash has been on the back or front pages three times. In the 1994 British Open, Pakistani Mir Zaman Gul was disqualified for headbutting Australian Anthony Hill at the old Lambs Club in London. After going 7-0 down in the decider, an incensed Gul threw his racket towards his opponent, eyeballed him from close quarters before Hill went down dramatically after the headbutt. Hill said afterwards: 'When he butted me, I thought 'that's nice, I'll sit down here and have the match, thank you'.' Then there was the furore over a world No 1 Scotsman who switched nationality to English (Peter Nicol in 2001), and a top woman player photographed posing in a thong on court to drum up publicity for the women's British Open.

The press need 'stories' about squash; results or great

matches simply aren't good enough. So far, we have heard nothing about the Games itself, nothing of the action that is destined to take place, potentially some of the greatest sport in the world. Because of the problems in Delhi, news of the Games is ubiquitous. The press are about as unforgiving as lions closing in on a helpless wilderbeast: ruthless, uncaring and hungry.

Which is just how I view some of my training sessions with my brother. This was always going to be one of my last chances at a really tough training day before leaving for Delhi so I went over to see him. The hardest sessions we do are the ones that give me the mental strength. After them, David often says: 'It's in the bank, little Jimbo. In the bank', to which the only reply I am capable is: 'I know. I know.'

SIX

THE COMMONWEALTHS, OUR PINNACLE

29 September 2010

Cameras greeted our entrance at Delhi airport, an unusual scenario for squash players at arrivals, although the Hollywood entrance has been laid on for us a couple of times in Pakistan, where interest in squash is high, because of that nation's illustrious history in the game.

The first drive through Delhi towards the Commonwealth Games epicentre gave an impression of disorganisation. Scaffolding was everywhere, engineering work was conducted through sheer manpower and hard labour, rather than expensive machinery and state of the art technology. There was a surprising abundance of space, which cannot not be said of Mumbai or especially Chennai, the Indian cities that I have previously visited. Green trees lined the roadside on the bus journey and I saw only a little of the impoverished living conditions that are synonymous with this country.

The gates of the village were upon us and we could clearly see the national flags hanging from apartment balconies, images familiar to us from the television pictures back home.

'Do we have any England flags to put on our balconies?' someone asked from the back of the bus jovially. 'No', replied Stafford Murray our manager. 'And if we did we wouldn't be allowed to'.

The England team are more of a target than anyone, and

for this reason there is to be no going outside of the village with team clothing on. In fact, we had been advised against going outside of the village at all.

At the gate came the first security checks, where the bus remained for a number of minutes to be probed diligently and it was clear to see that the long journey wouldn't be over for a while.

There will be plenty more security checks over the next few weeks.

30 September 2010

The village here in Delhi is a bubble of excitement, a legoland town standing alone just half a mile from a river upon which families settle and live under sheets of tarpaulin.

The imperfections are evident: areas are cordoned off; chiefs talk to Indian workers in a way that makes it clear that a caste system still exists in some form here; the odd yellow brick tile on paths is loose and there is no such thing as 'health and safety'. Marble areas of the path are dusty and slippery, and lawns outside the living quarters could have looked pristine, but instead lie bare in patches. At night there is a hush and loud music blurts from a nearby makeshift stage – all of it slightly reminiscent of a music festival at 3am. Mosquitoes hug street lamps and boxers run past in threes attempting to shed weight. They run like they are boxing, punching the air as they swing their arms in such a way that seems choreographed to get attention.

Practically speaking, there is everything anyone would need: a post office, a barber, an outdoor cinema, all sorts of shops. A foot massage is available should an athlete need some pampering, and there is even a bar and a disco. The 24-hour food hall is a hive of activity and it offers different foods from around the world.

The squash centre isn't a let down. The championship court has enough seating for thousands, and is one of the best venues I have seen. As in Melbourne, at the first sight of the arena, a warm glow prevails and a surge of adrenalin kicks in. This reaction reminds me of the deep affection I have for squash and the life it has provided me with. Viewing a sporting arena like this knowing that I will compete within it makes every practice hit, every session, worthwhile.

There's plenty of media interest here, too. Just walking through the village, three or four journalists approach me. I watch the inspirational montage that Will Forbes, our analyst, made for us. I hardly knew that I was so capable of inspiring myself, but somehow he has eked out from the archives my greatest rallies, and put them against my favourite music. A good touch and one for each member of the team.

During the night I hear all sorts of scraping coming from above my room. At first I am convinced it is rats, and that would almost be a relief; I would prefer rats to snakes any day. After 10 minutes of this racket I walk upstairs to the next floor, and the apartment directly above is inhabited by the coaching staff. Upon opening the hallway door I see an exasperated Stafford Murray, flanked by half a dozen Indian workmen. Parts of the toilet are in the communal areas, in an attempt to clear a bad drainage problem, and there is dirty water everywhere.

'I asked for this to be sorted three days ago. They've decided to turn up now, of all times', dead-pans Stafford.

'What, at 1am? Welcome to India.' We chuckle. Not really an awful lot else to say. We all agree that this sort of thing is part of the deal here in India, and that we will have to be accepting.

* * *

The Opening ceremony

Hoards of participants and coaches gathered on the paths outside the apartments in anticipation of the opening ceremony. For many athletes it presents a dilemma: some avoid it so as to concentrate on their competition, some like to soak up the experience. The problem lies in the fact that it is no small operation and to convene hundreds of athletes in the right place at the right time is a difficult proposition. There is half a day of sitting around to endure for that five minutes of excitement and glamour in the stadium.

Meeting at 3:45 and arriving back at the village six hours later made it a protracted affair. However, the journey to the stadium was relatively painless and a two hour wait in a holding area just outside sounds worse than it was.

The last hour preceding the parade was a drag though, as all participants were led *en masse* up to the entrance of the stadium through a sweltering tunnel. It was crowded and hot and there came a point where the heat became almost unbearable. Initially it was funny, but by the time the stadium and its glare was upon us, it had become painful. Adrian Grant's pretty Indian uniform was soaked with sweat, and I'm surprised nobody fainted. The only athletes who would have benefited from it were the boxers who would have undoubtedly made their weights.

7 October 2010

It has been some day. I beat David Palmer in arguably one of the most important matches we have played. It was scheduled for 7:30 in the evening, already a late shift. The match between Madeleine Perry and Kasey Brown went to five and my team-mate Daryl Selby and Malaysian Aslan

Iskandar's scrap, in which all hell broke loose, lasted around two hours. Palmer and I ended up taking to the court at around 10:30pm.

The mental pressure all this deploys is enormous: as the hours sauntered by, I felt sure I had never warmed up so many times before a match. I had practically played a match. Daryl's game was a see-saw affair and I couldn't gauge the timing. In the end he lost in a titanic struggle which culminated with a dead leg injury and cramps, both suffered by the Englishman.

My match with Palmer proceeded in similar fashion. He came out firing and played a high tempo game, almost catching me by surprise – last time we played back in August the pace had been slower – albeit on a bouncier court.

The court was causing problems, more for me than him, and during the second game I decided I couldn't take any more. The court floor didn't seem to be absorbing the sweat and I reached the point where I didn't want to risk it anymore. At 8-10 down I slipped, stopped and asked for a let ball, which was perhaps unfairly given to me, but I just couldn't carry on and felt that my efforts to continue the match in such conditions had merited the replaying of the rally.

Palmer came off and argued that it should never be a let, I came off and simultaneously declared that I was not prepared to carry on; a crowd made up of English and Aussie managers and coaches gathered around the glass court to argue with the tournament referee and tournament director. After much disagreement I was left with no choice but to either carry on or forfeit the match, since both players would have to agree to the change of courts. It was hardly surprising that at 1-0 and 10-8 up Palmer wanted to stay on there.

As it happened, things did get a little better: I changed

all of my clothing, which seemed to be holding the sweat, and I tucked my shirt in to my shorts to stem the flow of fluid on to the floor. Since I was the heaviest sweater, this strategy seemed to help.

I lost the second but coming back on in the third I found the problem had reduced slightly. I had not played fluently all night, and realised soon enough that I was going to have to depend on every bit of toughness I had built over my years of experience.

As the third began I contained him a little better, not pressing in short quite as often. The rallies were now ultra punishing and I had to keep on finding strength from somewhere. Lots of reaching, lots of lunging. There were less stoppages for court wiping, and I started to feel his intensity drop, ever so slightly.

The quality and pace of his play in the first two were so ferocious that I remember thinking there must be a drop at some stage. Up and down the backhand wall we went, brushing past each other in such proximity, quite unique to the game of squash and I could occasionally hear his deep breathing. Receiving serve I remember at one point we caught one another's eye and I noticed an air of disturbed discomfort, bordering on panic on his face, with sweat pouring down each cheek as he prepared to serve.

I hoped I was making a better job of not showing my pain as he did his, but I doubted that. We had been here so many times, in this gruelling position in major championships, locked in battle. At 5-1 down in the fourth I hit another wall. I was struggling physically, which was puzzling considering I had felt fit and fresh coming into the event, having had a backlog of heavy sessions under my belt. Perhaps I did too much in the run up.

Facing a disappointing exit from the event I had worked so hard for, I took four points in a row to get back to parity, before pulling away only slightly to take the match in to a fifth. It felt like a lifeline I didn't quite deserve. As I won the final point of that game Palmer made one of his desperate trademark dives in to the corner and I knew the balance had tipped, a result of my forcing him to manoeuvre his thick set body more and more. I heard a roar from my manager Mick in the crowd, a sound I associate with success and pleasure. I had to do it now.

Palmer then took some time out for a blood injury. I didn't concern myself with it, but instead hit balls on the court to keep my eye in and keep moving. I swung my racket listlessly, thinking how horribly hard even this small movement felt. Taking a break, as much as I wanted to, would have made it worse.

Back in play I sensed a more considerable drop in energy on his part. Having gone two points down I then pulled away to 6-2 and I started to feel him weakening somewhat. Ironically, he was now slipping and complaining about the floor. The kit changes I had made definitely helped matters, although the court was nowhere near perfect and I still would have asked for the cleaners a few times, had David advised me not to. If I could get Palmer to ask for the court cleaning, it would prove that he deemed the court unfit for play which would result in a change of court, according to the rules as they had been dictated by tournament director Andrew Shelley in the fracas at the end of the second.

As Palmer slipped in the fifth, he left pools of sweat all over the floor which required the attention of the busy court cleaners. During one such break I saw my opponent downing energy gels in his corner through the glass wall. At seeing this I was sure I had the match in the bag until a matter of rallies later, at 9-4 up, my left quad tightened heavily, threatening cramp. I wasn't aware that Palmer may have already been suffering from cramp, something David told me after the match, and every movement I made with that left leg had to be made with extreme trepidation. To anyone who hasn't experienced the onset, it is practically impossible not to show the pain when it sets in. I was in a precarious position. If the cramp really took hold, I would not be able to move, and would almost certainly lose, despite having a good lead.

The match had been monstrously hard and, having had everything from arguments between managers to cramping and diving, we both stood spent, eking out those last rallies of the fifth past midnight in downtown Delhi. Almost simultaneously, we found ourselves hitting massive weak spells, brick walls. It seemed that we were both desperately trying not to show the other how much physical discomfort we were going through.

On the winning point I triumphantly turned to the bench, all of whom were in uproar. I had managed to stave off cramp and take myself closer to a medal. Whatever happens now, this match will take some beating for the levels of squash, drama and excitement.

Coming off court, I knew almost immediately my night was not over. Having already conceded that I wouldn't sleep for hours, I was assured that this period of time would be elongated when a man with a clip board approached me. It was 1am. There is nothing like a drug test to burst the bubble of success, and they could have hardly chosen a worse time. I had lost litres of sweat, and there was no way I would be able to provide urine for hours. There is nothing to do in this situation but get on with it. Physio Phil took care of my body for an hour or two, whilst I drank and drank, and ate, in an effort to refuel as well as possible for the semi final the following evening.

Phil and I had a rewarding evening/morning together, one that will always be remembered for its surrealism if nothing else, where we talked and laughed and ate in the eerily quiet food hall at 4am. My head was on the pillow an hour later.

7 October 2010

Since getting up this morning all I have done is eat, sleep and doze intermittently. The mental build up to yesterday and the match itself has taken a toll, and I haven't once considered tonight's match, which should I win will get me a silver medal at least. Fretting and focusing too hard on today wouldn't help.

8 October 2010

I woke to feel excitement and anticipation at the prospect of playing the Commonwealth Games gold medal match. I spent only 43 minutes on court against Azlan Iskandar, of Malaysia. We were both trying to make the best of the situation, languishing after being on court the previous night for two hours-plus in our respective quarter finals.

9 October 2010

The gold medal match against Nick didn't go my way. I was disappointed to lose 3-0 after a match of high intensity and quality. The experience was phenomenal. The crowd were about 1500 strong and created a great atmosphere. The England camp covered the front row, a sight to behold for everyone involved with English squash, and we were pleased that we had come away with four of the six possible singles medals.

After the final there was a flurry of interviews and press conferences. Nick and I were immediately thrown into the glare of the media and were interviewed by Matt Pinsent for the BBC. While my Pontefract friends and supporters waited to see me, the media took priority, and they had left by the time I finished the interviews. I regret letting that happen in the way it did. Those supporters are dependable and that can't always be said for the press.

I was asked to do my second drugs test of the week. Again I was the last person out of the complex, and I took a lone bus ride home, disappointed. It was another big comedown, the thought of trying to go to sleep filled me with fear.

The newspapers that were lying about on the bus were full of Commonwealth Games reports. The front pages talked of logistical matters, matters of infrastructure and legacy, criticism, ticket sales; the back pages of results and reports of the games. I flicked through, slightly uninterested. I had had enough. As I came to the end of the sports pages, which told of results and especially the home heroes who were making India proud and how athletes were 'so thrilled' to achieve a personal best or to be an inspiration, my eyes diverted quickly to the adjacent page, on which the headline read 'Hue and Cry' notice. I did not know what these notices entailed, so I read on. I began to realise that it was a notice to appeal to a family or friend to identify the body of someone deceased. Someone, during those last few days, while thousands of athletes had been preparing to perform to their sporting best, had died in terrible circumstances, and had died alone. I was shocked to find the page had photos of dead bodies. Should no one claim kinship of these people, what would become of them?

India has always seemed to highlight the divide between luxury and austerity, rich and poor, ornate and plain. Five star hotels exist in areas where extreme poverty is rife. It hardly seems right that the Games organisers should spend millions on an inflatable flying buggy for the opening ceremony, or that because we are good athletes we should be shielded from the dire conditions in which people must live here in Delhi.

The dining hall was curiously quiet in the early hours. I rang Vanessa and Malc before going back to the apartment. Despite being happy with the performance, I found it difficult to switch off, the contrasts of the last six or seven hours too difficult to fathom. So many thoughts, but finally I caught some sleep at around 5am.

10 October 2010

I have been reading with interest Matt Pinsent's blog in which he acknowledges the incredible success of the England squash team here in Delhi. There is general confusion as to why the game, unlike the other major racket sports, still hasn't made it on to the Olympic programme. Many people are incredulous when they find out it isn't included; 'Really? Squash isn't an Olympic sport? And tennis is?' I am asked about squash and the Olympics more than anything else and struggle to come up with an answer.

The sport has been fighting long and hard for Games recognition and has come extremely close, most notably for London 2012. In Singapore in 2005 – when London won the 2012 bid – squash was one of two sports put forward after baseball and softball were ejected. However, squash and karate both failed to obtain the IOC's controversial two-thirds majority vote. I remember watching the television for the result after a training session at Pontefract. I found it impossible not to project ahead; if all went well, at 29-years-old, a prime age for a squash player, I had a big chance of not only competing in the first ever squash event at the Olympics, but of doing so in London, in my home country.

The IOC amended its charter for the 2016 vote and only a single majority was deemed necessary. However, we barely even came close and golf and rugby sevens were recommended.

The inclusion of golf in the Rio Games seemed to baffle many people I spoke to around the time. It seems inevitable that the money and celebrity that golf can provide was a deciding factor, and these two words cannot be readily used to describe squash. Perhaps the lure of Rory McIlroy and Tiger Woods was too much to turn down.

As with tennis and football – major sports which have enjoyed Olympic involvement at the expense of others – I predict the world's best golfers will not consider the Olympic event their greatest and most prestigious one, as most of the other sports do, and as squash would.

The great Jahangir Khan put it like this: 'It will be the biggest honour and the highest accolade for squash players to feature in an Olympic spectacle.' Jahangir is absolutely right.

Our next chance is for the 2020 games, which will be decided at IOC sessions in 2013. Despite my faltering hopes, I maintain that squash is deserving of a place in the globe's largest sporting festival. It would undoubtedly give the sport a generous boost in the UK, considering our present potential for winning Olympic medals and the media exposure that follows.

Indeed squash seems to cry out the words 'Olympic ethos': a truer all round sport combining fitness, skill, agility, speed, strength, flexibility, focus and guile cannot be found. It is accessible to kids on the street and city businessmen alike, is portable (a glass court can be put just about anywhere) and incredibly healthy. Most importantly, it is universally played in countries all over the world; 150 countries are affiliated to the WSF. The professional game thrives; the PSA world tour now stages 10 world series events a year, with each boasting over $100,000 in player prize money. It is also consistently attracting healthy crowds of spectators not only at the events themselves but online. Let us not be in doubt that the game is watchable.

Unfortunately though, one thing that certainly hasn't been watchable is the doubles here in Delhi and I have no qualms in saying that it has been an appalling spectacle. The game can be summed up as a constant barrage of backcourt squash, which needs to either be radically changed or scrapped all together. Its present format is ruinous and the sport as a whole will suffer because of it.

13 October 2010

Jenny Duncalf and I failed to make our seeding in the mixed doubles, losing in the quarter finals to Cameron Pilley and Kasey Brown, of Australia. Nevertheless, England's doubles campaign ended on a high after Jenny and Laura Massaro took silver in the women's event and Adrian and Nick took gold in the men's event.

After all the high-fiving and smiling, the posing for photographs and the watching, we were transported *en masse* to the team lodge where a pleasant occasion ensued, with beer and champagne and celebratory speeches from managers, players, coaches and families. England had topped the medal table for squash. I was quite surprised that the barman didn't get up and say a few words, such was the general feeling of joviality in the room. We declared that we were a unit and that that was what had brought us through. Despite the team success I could not help but feel at odds with the general celebrations.

A few of us took a bus back to the village. In a thick Delhi dusk we ambled to the food hall, medals clunking, for one last ice cream. There were none left. Indecisively, we all parted, and the Commonwealth Games, an event that had demanded so much of our attention and focus over the last year, was over.

Almost two weeks to the hour we had arrived in Delhi, fresh and urgent. Now I sit in the apartment, the Games over, deflated. Everyone else has gone. I look to the floor and see adidas kit strewn about the place. The same kit that two weeks previously had symbolised hope and opportunity is now useless and will soon be relegated to a loft.

On the wall are blu-tacked sheets displaying practice schedules, maps and important telephone numbers, all of which formed the direction of our lives only days ago. Team England posters emblazon the walls. 'We are proud' they say, and 'we are ambitious'.

I think back to Melbourne and remember that I've been here before. There's a come down every other week at present, but the Commonwealth Games come downs are more intense. In Melbourne, the feelings of anti-climax were abated somewhat because of an immediate trip to beautiful Bermuda. This time though, we have Egypt to look forward to.

SEVEN

STARTING TO SLIDE

15 October 2010

Tired and ill, I entered the arrivals hall in Alexandria airport to complete chaos. Passport control had four lines that merged into one, and there wasn't the slightest semblance of order. After negotiation of the passport control from hell, a visa had to be purchased across the other side of the hall – from a man in a booth with a computer from the 1980s – which involved a dog fight through crowds of rambunctious Arabs. I paid the man my dues only to have to fight my way back through again to retrieve the passport which the visa would now validate. This is a country that doesn't do systems.

Upon arrival at the Hilton, after being ripped off in the taxi, neither caring or knowing what price to even barter for, I waited for a room at check in for an hour and a half. I couldn't vent as strongly as I wished to as the beautiful receptionist repeatedly told me they were doing everything they could to accommodate me. Once I was finally given a room, I enjoyed a glorious nap and woke up at around 3, just in time for the 3:07 'call to prayer', which reverberated around the hotel complex from the mosque nearby. Soon after I took a call from the manager asking if we would like a change of room as the disco downstairs could sometimes be disturbing at night. I thanked him for his concern and moved.

After a jacuzzi in the hotel spa, from which I soon fled after being repeatedly stared at, Saurav arrived and we pathetically attempted to practice.

I had been looking forward to a sleep that evening, but all hopes were shattered at 4:37am when yet another call to prayer blared from a nearby tannoy adjacent to the hotel, unbelievably within striking distance of our room. As I charged down to the lobby, bleary eyed and incensed, I didn't really think about how my complaint was going to be received. The hotel staff weren't going to be able to do anything; they certainly weren't going to call up the mosque to say that Mr. James had complained and ask if the prayers could be kept to a minimum.

Why were they praying in the middle of the night, and could they not at least keep it to themselves? The receptionists certainly weren't bothering to pray and none of the Muslim squash players seemed to be rushing to the mosque at 4:30am. What tragic irony it was that Allah seemed to be communicating only with me, one of the few who wouldn't listen. There was no evidence of any disco. That would have been preferable.

18 October 2010

I went down to the club in good time so that I could check that the courts were in order. The floors were slippery yesterday and I helped mop and sweep them. I wondered if Novak Djokovic cleaned the tennis court before play in a Grand Slam. It's all part of the charm of squash, though. It's the inaugural El Gouna International event, and one or two teething issues are to be expected. As players we can often help or advise with respect to court maintenance or other logistical issues.

Later I decided to watch some of the Egyptian coaches in action with their juniors. As I sat watching, an affable young man came and introduced himself. Strangely and unusually for an Egyptian, he seemed to know who I was.

'Hello Willstrop. I am Mina. I like your game. I watch videos.'

'Thank you. Good to meet you.'

'I play you.' Note the absence of a question mark.

'No I am playing soon.'

'You play me later. I will be on court one if you want.'

'No I have a match to play, sorry', I said, amazed at his audacity. What next? Would he charge me for coming on court with him?

Waiting for my match later still I watched a young boy, of about 10, being flogged to death by his coach. The latter persistently shouted at the boy to work harder as he forced him to do tiring ghosting exercises. I had no idea that this was the way they worked in Egypt, and there will be little chance for that particular child, working so hard at such an age. Any traces of love that boy has for squash are being sucked away by his pushy coach. The boy's mother, who sat outside the court watching, expressionless, was clearly unaware of the damage being inflicted. If Egyptian kids are getting so good by doing that, they can keep their junior trophies.

As the matches began, utter chaos ensued. Three courts were used for all the matches, and there were people everywhere. John Massarella, international referee, was flapping about trying to find referees while players waited, warmed up and ready to play. At one point John was adjudicating a match using the three-referee system, with a PSA player as the right ref, and an Egyptian 'local' as the left ref. The local positioned himself in line with the join of the adjacent court and so could see the play on both. At one point he became confused, or so absorbed in the other match, that he gave a decision for that match, the wrong one, putting his hand up signalling a let, causing perplexity all around. John, as the central ref on the correct court, had not been expecting a decision and wondered why his referee had signalled for one in the middle of a rally.

19 October 2010

The chest was still tight today and I didn't feel anywhere near 100 per cent during my first round match. Thankfully I got through in three, a bonus. We collectively flew to El Gouna today, a holiday resort, where the rest of the tournament will be played out on a glass court.

True to form, the journey was disorganised and chaotic. Personnel at Alexandria Airport didn't seem too bothered about security; some players were given boarding passes labelled under the names of other PSA players, who weren't even playing in the event! Imagine that at Heathrow.

21 October 2010

Arrived back at my room at 1am after the conditions of the court intermittently made it unplayable all evening. Last match on, I won 3-0, at which time the court seemed to have settled. There were several stoppages during the evening, which explains the late finish. The disarray continues.

22 October 2010

I conceded my quarter final match with Greg. I couldn't stand up on the slippery court. It appears that sand had found its way on to the court because of the stronger winds. Greg said it was bad, but not so bad that we needed to stop the match. I don't blame him necessarily, but I clearly struggled with the situation more than he did, or maybe I was the one who, after a lot of squash, wasn't prepared to risk breaking my neck.

26 October 2010
Kuwait Open, Kuwait City

The culture in Kuwait is not one that many westerners would instantly warm to – the oppression and segregation of women, the censoring of absolutely anything remotely explicit, lack of alcohol, possible terror threats, the incessant and wholehearted belief in God – but despite these issues, the Kuwait Open has always been one of the most enjoyable and well organised tournaments to come to. Kuwait is clean, the weather is good and the event is run with aplomb.

As I adjusted to the surroundings before the tournament proper, I perused the shops at the Marina Mall. I walked away empty handed. I have too much luggage as it is and resisted the temptation of buying a cheap copy of Dickens' *The Mystery of Edwin Drood*.

I watched my training partner Saurav play Egyptian Wael El Hindi. Saurav was disappointed with his performance, quite rightly, as his standard is undoubtedly on a par, but Wael is skilful and clever, and with experience behind him can be hard to beat.

El Hindi threw in a couple of blocks at the end of the match, and so in an amiable sort of way, I put a question to the referee afterwards: 'Did you see Hindi's movement at 4-4? Did you see the deliberate movement he made?'

'Ah, it was too good, and Saurav wouldn't have got the ball.' So he clearly hadn't seen it.

Daryl Selby, who had been seated close by and was equally frustrated by the referee's tendency not to penalise blocking, came in on the conversation, reiterating my feelings. We repeated ourselves, but he couldn't grasp it. Moments later, as I waited for the bus, I glanced towards the tournament office and clapped eyes on Daryl, who was flying off in a rage and shouting at somebody there.

The altercation was heated and the ref he was talking to, rather than listen to what Daryl had to say, became defensive, stating at one point that deliberate blocking is part of the game.

The reason we want to share our feelings is to help the referees, nothing else. The players don't know it all. We are not criticising to be vindictive, but to increase understanding. The players realise that the referees don't know what it is like playing world level matches (we players don't know what it is like to referee world level matches) and so there are things both parties can offer to each other. To shut off and not be accepting of a player's comments is not wise, and it is only natural to lose respect for someone who reacts in this way.

There are three second round matches at the club in downtown Kuwait. The atmosphere is muted, the club empty. The back court matches always stand in contrast to the glamour and the big occasion of playing on the glass in the main arena further down the coast. With everything in place, the kit ready and time to spare, the venue and the atmosphere doesn't quite do justice to the importance of the competition here today. Yorkshire League matches at Pontefract can be more stimulating.

It isn't time to warm-up – the game before is dragging – so what to do but sit and feel nervous? This match feels extra important because of the fact that I am seeded to meet Karim Darwish in the quarters – of late it has been exclusively Nick and Ramy – so it is an opening, albeit a small one.

I beat Mohamed El Shorbagy in four games.

31 October 2010

Darwish starts well, playing with force and conviction. Despite a convincing 11-5 scoreline in his favour, I battle hard to engage him in physical spells and I know he must feel the pace. On winning the game he shouts 'come on', as he often does, and this is enough to tell me he did not find it easy.

The second is tough again. We labour down the backhand wall, teasing each other to make movements neither of us is that happy to make – this is the nature of squash at the highest level.

The end of each rally reminds me of the heat, as I wipe my hand subconsciously on the back wall glass, attempting to rid myself of excess sweat. From as early as the third I am aware that the increase in temperature is sapping every drop of energy away. After levelling at 1-1, I win the third easily as he starts to weaken; the fourth runs well for him, and never really starts for me, though unlike his effort a game ago, I am sure to hang in, telling myself that the more I push him now the more benefit I will get in the fifth.

I lead for most of the fifth, keeping a couple of points up on him at all times. Just as we have another brutal rally, I squeeze an error to maintain that lead. And it is a squeeze. Because of the conditions to which neither of us is accustomed, at every rally's end I feel each heartbeat crashing into my rib cage, and I tell myself to go through 10 more minutes with a view to jumping into a bucket of ice and spending a day in bed. It is incredible to think that an extra few degrees of heat can make squash that much harder. I close out the match 11-6 to set up a semi final with Ramy Ashour.

1 November 2010

Playing Ramy. Where do we start with this?

Standing on the same court facing the young Egyptian –

who won the World Open aged 21 – at any time is some test, and playing him with an 85-minute match from the previous day lingering in the legs is enough to cause great apprehension. He has the ability to dismantle the very best players. To face him off the back of one of the hardest matches of the season might well be double trouble. I go into the match with slight trepidation but am relaxed enough.

Ramy is quite simply the most unusual squash player I have ever seen or been on court with. The matches I play against fellow professionals, let's say, can be thrown in to one category, which could be labelled 'normal squash'. Ramy, though, has invented a new category and one most of us hardly knew was attainable before he came along. For those who have been lucky enough to see him play, we all know how able he is with a racket – those backhand cross-court nicks are sublime – but what is more staggering is the pace at which he is constantly inclined to play, with regard to both his movement, court coverage, and his racket head speed through the ball.

I'm sure any one of the top 10 players would be happy to admit that the pace of his game operates on a different plane. It doesn't make him unbeatable or even necessarily the best player, but to consider winning against him, squash of the highest calibre is required.

Anyone who has been (un)lucky enough to step on court with him will know, his game operates at such a speed that it can make any player in the world look silly. Because of the speed he generates through the wrist and arm, the ball travels faster and with more zip. It sounds as though anyone could probably achieve this in time. You can't. I think we've all probably secretly tried – and to date, failed.

His movement, anticipation and racket speed is great enough that he can play the simplest of straight drop shots and with his natural deception, have a world-class player bolting to the opposite corner, in the most ungainly manner.

The Egyptian would be an interesting study for those who have read *The Talent Code* by Daniel Coyle or *Bounce* by Matthew Syed, the former table tennis player turned journalist. The general theme of those books is that success is always achieved as a result of the practice and commitment an athlete puts into his or her sport over a great many months and years. Undoubtedly Ramy practises hitting those nicks endlessly, and he is a hard worker, but I feel there is something especially innate with regards to his ability.

Without knowing a lot about his methods I would hazard a guess that his training is hard but not particularly scientific. I can't believe he has any secret formula that I or other top players don't know about. If anything, westerners are likely to have better strength and conditioning coaches, physios and physical support. Ramy intermittently makes visits to England for his physiotherapy treatment because of the lack of top people in the field in Egypt, which is what leads me to believe that his speed and astounding ability is derived, in part, from his natural capabilities. Of course, hard work, as those books rightly point out, is very much part of the equation, as it is for Usain Bolt, to whom, unsurprisingly, Ramy is frequently compared. Neither of these superstar athletes would have achieved anything without the hard work, but perhaps I could suggest that their talent, or the make-up of their DNA, plays a *more* significant role in their success than it does with many other athletes.

At each one of his matches, there is always a smattering of players present. I have watched him a great deal, and am still left breathless by what he can do on a squash court. I can never see enough.

Not only does his play carry so much obvious aesthetic appeal but the personality and the charisma he exudes is also really positive for the game. Every time I sit in the crowd to watch a match of his, I look at the audience, who are always reacting to something he is doing: his talking to himself, his tip-toe movement before receiving serve or the humorous dialogue with the referees.

The man goes relatively unannounced globally, which is a terrible injustice. He is undoubtedly one of the greatest sportsmen on the planet – certainly the most talented holding a racket – and to think most sports fans in this country know more about lower league football is so sad.

The same goes for Amr Shabana. Shabana's four major wins in two months in 2007 is regarded in squash circles as a truly mammoth achievement. Not only is the man the most artistic hitter of a squash ball that has ever been, and a true gentleman, he is also a winner. He stands, justifiably, as a legend of the sport.

Likewise, for Nick to come off court after our two hour Canary Wharf match and then front up to beat a top 10 player 24 hours later in the final was one of the most staggering athletic endeavours I can recall, yet nobody seemed to really bat an eyelid. Perhaps I am best placed to commend Nick's effort that week because I was involved, and therefore understand what it feels like to play one match of that quality, let alone two within 24 hours. When do marathon runners or boxers or footballers or 800 metre runners ever compete against a rival in the most intense race of their lives, and then repeat it a day later and win? The answer, of course, is never, and that is not wishing to decry their efforts.

So it is safe to say that I don't go into this match with massive expectations. I warm-up gingerly in the heat and the ball flies about in the first game. I am almost a little surprised at the end of it to feel myself starting to move quite freely. After losing it 11-7 I find my way back into the match, winning the second. I am unable to take enough fluid on board, (for some reason I feel bloated) which is not helpful considering the oppressive heat. Nevertheless the play is good.

In the third the intensity starts to crank up. The hot conditions begin to tell, and I can see that he is affected because there is a greater delay than usual in between his serves. After I take a 6-1 lead he suddenly makes me feel like I've forgotten how to win a rally again, getting back to 6-7. It's a patchy end to an imbalanced third which ends 11-9 in his favour.

I make a good start in the fourth, responding well. Again he replies positively but this time when he brings himself back level I don't panic, remaining calm and staying with him. The pace is furious; for some reason there are too many lets, which is threatening to put a dampener on a quality game. We take turns to score points as the scoreboard flows again, staying neck and neck until he holds a match ball at the business end, 10-9.

Pleasingly, I manage to respond, now silently pleading for air to enter my lungs, such is the intensity of the battle. I win my game ball at 11-10 with a clinger on the left wall, and we are level at 2-2, a scenario I would have gladly taken beforehand.

I start promisingly in the fifth but halfway through, Ramy unfortunately for me, decides to raise the bar, swatting nicks all over the court. This great spell gives him a four point cushion, and the end of this particular contest is soon upon me when he builds on his lead, zipping around the court with renewed vigour, racing to 9-4. He wins the fifth convincingly, but only after more breakneck rallies, and I made sure the foot stayed on the throttle.

We shake hands and I sit by the side of the court, as spent as I can remember but highly encouraged that I am able to put my body through two world-class matches in two nights, and to have played so well.

EIGHT

THE MAIN EVENT
30 November 2010
World Open, Saudi Arabia

Had an early start this morning, leaving the hotel in central London at 7am. Last night's taxi driver, an Iraqi in whom Mick had total faith, despite Malc's and my own reservations, was asked to turn up for us this morning and deliver us to the airport. Mick, to whom the glass is always half full gave the bloke a chance and he didn't turn up. Not a good start really, for which Mick was heavily criticised, but fortunately we were able to fall back on the efficiency of the hotel staff, who organised a cab at the last minute.

Reaching Bahrain from home via trains, plane and then crossing the border to Saudi, takes a day and a half. Our destination for the next 10 days is Al-Khobar and Sunset Beach, a resort on Saudi's east coast. The biggest tournament is here thanks to the efforts of Ziad Al-Turki, the men's world tour chairman. The charismatic Ziad, whose uncle had a squash court built in his house, has injected funds into the sport and squash is beginning to see the effects.

I received a text from David saying that he had missed out on the National coaches job for England Squash and Racketball, which knocks me off my kilter somewhat. I thought that his past within the association might have brought him through. Chris Robertson has been given the job. Chris is a highly respected former world number two, and has been the Welsh coach for the last fifteen years. I have always enjoyed listening to his commentaries on Sky Sports, and wish him well in his new role.

I am due to play Nicolas Mueller, of Switzerland, in the first round. Lower-ranked players against top eight players often treat the first round as their Cup final, putting in every ounce of energy. Pair this with an often general rustiness of the higher-ranked player after two or three weeks without competition and it means there is a match on. I always remember Peter Nicol having problems in his first rounds even when he was at the very top of his game. He said they required as much focus as a final.

I will need to apply this mentality for my match. Mueller is improving all the time and I am almost certain he is the toughest last 64 draw. It will also be our first meeting on tour.

4 December 2010

As expected, last night's match was tough but I played well to win 3-1. I'm thankful for the day off, too. Tonight I played fluently to beat Borja Golan. However, I ended the match feeling insecure about a slight niggle in my right thigh. Around the World Open I continuously live life on the edge, almost waiting for things to happen. But I'm feeling good here and hopefully I can rid myself of it.

No sooner had I finished than I saw Ramy was 9-0 down in the second against Aamir Atlas. Minutes later he had retired because of a hamstring injury. He is devastated and everybody feels for him, but almost simultaneously, at the moment I hear Ramy is out, I begin to think of my shaky thigh and the doubts come back to the surface. Ramy's exit shows how fragile we all are considering the nature of the game. People are already insinuating that his being out of the tournament cuts a path for me to the semis, but I am far too preoccupied with the thigh to think like that.

7 December 2010

The tournament has kicked in for real now. I played Daryl Selby in what turned out to be a protracted encounter. Giving Daryl, a world top 10 player, the slightest sniff spells disaster. After my good start he had me under pressure in the second with consistent spells of accuracy and tightness, especially down the left wall. I reasserted to take the third and led 7-3 in the fourth, almost thinking I was there. I couldn't have been more wrong as he embarked on his strongest physical spell of the match. At 6-7 we had a hard rally that left me cursing under my breath as I wiped my hand on the back wall, incredulous that he had been able to respond with such tenacity. Despite the discomfort, I had a feeling that this sort of push could not be sustained by him for much longer. I edged back in to the lead and eventually closed out the match.

In the post match interview I conveyed my relief at getting through the match in four rather than five. More importantly though, I was pleased with the leg. I hadn't felt it.

8 December 2010

The less I think about how many minutes I have accumulated on court the better. I avoid reading any reports with this in mind. I suppose I am thinking that a match as hard as the one against Daryl can only hinder my chances of winning the world title. I can't really afford to be having such tough matches in the last 16. The energy is needed for the later rounds. Karim, Nick, Greg and Shabana all remain unscathed up until now.

In many respects, the hard match may take a little bit of

pressure off. Ever since, I have ceased to think about the end result of being world champion. I just have to concentrate on beating Mohamed El Shorbagy in the last eight.

* * *

What a difference a day makes. The previous night I lay jaded on the physio's couch thinking how the match with Daryl could have damaged my chances of winning here. Now, 24 hours later, I lie on my bed having disposed of Shorbagy in under an hour to be facing another team-mate Peter Barker – and not Darwish, who had conceded after a heavy fall on court – for a place in a World Open final. Gaultier also conceded with an injury, and I heard both were terrible. I felt for the two boys and of course for Ramy, who must be struggling to see their dreams fragment in such a way. But I now have every chance.

I was galvanised by my clinical display tonight. I coped with the high pace of Shorbagy's game, going with him at times but breaking up the rhythms when necessary. I knew it was a big opening, but he had beaten me last year in India so I was under no illusions as to how tough it would be. I won 3-0 in just under an hour.

I am using the evenings to switch off and relax, either with Mick and Malc at dinner, or by watching films and reading. The next match seems far enough away that I can temporarily forget about hitting that little black ball. The days are so intense that every morning brings another hangover.

9 December 2010

I wake after a pill-induced sleep and the first thought is that England have three out of the four semi-finalists. The second is that I am one of them. I go to the court at lunchtime for half an hour's hit, and immediately after coming off a feverishness hits me. All the work and all the days of training I've done, only to be stopped on the cusp by something external. In many respects, it is not surprising: the body is on the brink, and at some point soon it will break. I have to somehow try to keep it going for two more weeks.

Feeling awful, I doze while Malc sits with me, probably a little concerned. I am walking a tightrope. As the afternoon goes by I begin to feel better, and manage to eat reasonably well. I return to bed in the hope of saving as many reserves as possible for tonight.

Peter gets the better start and takes a lead. I am trying to feel my way around, preoccupied with thoughts of having a virus in my system. It becomes apparent that although I am not tip-top, I'm not feeling too bad. However, long rallies are harder than they would usually be and I am struggling to push on to the ball with any pace. (Later, Mick tells me that Vanessa texted him to ask what was wrong, recognising that there was a distinct lack of urgency; I had told her nothing so it must have been noticeable from the outside).

The psychology is difficult in this situation. I don't feel great, but neither do I feel bad; just physically off the boil. There is no way I can justify coming off in such a big match. So, after a minor whinge to Malc before the second game, I make a deal with myself to forget about any ailments and push as hard as I can for every point. If damage is to be done and if I really am ill then I might as well kill myself in the World Open semi-final. If I can't dig to the bottom of the well here then I may as well not bother, and I would be devastated if I let this opportunity go because of feeling a bit under the weather.

I get on with it, concentrating hard on every rally. From 10-

9 down in the second I manage to win the game 13-11. I am galvanised by the scoreboard: 1-1 is decisively different to 2-0.

The momentum is now with me. I almost control the third, and my plan of thinking about one rally at a time seems to be working. I am taking tiny footsteps and it helps. I draw away and win the third convincingly. I am transformed from feeling very negative to very positive within the space of half an hour, and now know that to carry this through and win is not only possible but likely. All thoughts of an illness are crushed in to oblivion by the magic that is adrenalin. I take the lead in the fourth and he comes back at me strongly before I close it out 11-8. The hands are aloft as if I am the champion. In fact, I think my hands have gone aloft after every match, such has been the significance of each one. I am in the World Open final and the trophy is within my sights. Funnily enough, Nick awaits. He beat Amr Shabana in three games. It's an all England, all Yorkshire final. Tomorrow one of us will be crowned the first ever English world champion.

After food with Mick and some chat (he talks to me in his positive and happy way, and I can tell in his voice that he could not be more behind me), I amble back to the cabanas with him, shake his hand, as I have done every night after dinner, and we part. 'You the man Jimbo, tomorrow', he drones deeply. I collapse onto the bed.

10 December 2010

This date has been significant for months now, the day of the final of the World Open. When the dates come out months or years before, a mental note is made in my head. Must...be...involved.

'That's the day of the World Open final. I want to be in it.'

In the weeks leading up to the tournament, plans are made and thoughts are attended to what will happen.

A certain perspective is maintained here though. For a start, I could be Darwish, Gaultier or Ramy, their dreams shattered in one fell swoop this year by injuries. Tonight I enter the court to play the biggest match in the sport. Whatever happens now, it is an occasion in which I am privileged to be involved. I wake up at 7:30am after about five hours' sleep, pop half a pill, and sleep again for another three hours. As has been the routine, I have breakfast and then meet Mick for a coffee at the café. I am doing things I enjoy with people I like, but thoughts of tonight gnaw at my belly. I forget for several minutes at a time, but soon enough the darts of nerves cut through me. A whole life's work goes in to performing well on this day and there are so few chances in which to win a world title. It is easy to comprehend why so much time is spent thinking about injuries or worrying about getting a shot right. To counteract this train of thought I tell myself that I have performed in all sorts of pressure situations, and have handled it well. I will do the same tonight.

Back in my room, I watch some television and put on the compex (a machine that physio Phil has given me to send electrical impulses through my leg). Malc comes over and we sit, chatting through the match and the approach. We watch the motivational DVD from the Commonwealth Games together. We walk to the coffee shop about an hour and a quarter before the final. I want a caffeine hit but the staff are too busy so we leave prematurely. I see Phil who tapes my feet and stretches my hips. Twenty minutes before the match I begin warming up, behind the scaffolding at the far side of the hall in which the court is housed, and instantly feel the tape rubbing on my feet.

That doesn't feel right!

Malc runs to get Phil, who brings the scissors. All done.

I begin again. Malc glares at my warm-up routine and intermittently throws in the odd comment. With 10 minutes to go the big screen begins to display a montage of all the World Open champions, with scenes of the winning rallies of this most prestigious event from years past. I don't know whether this is a good or bad thing; fascinated as I am, I can't help but watch a few snippets and the music and the images almost make me want to scream with excitement.

Five minutes to go and I take the final lavatory break. The bandanna and the wrist band are on. Racket ready. Body warm. I stand round the back and the compère hails a monumental occasion, in which two Englishmen will play the world final for the first time. I keep coming unstuck against Nick, so the last thing I want to do here is clutter my mind with a complex tactical approach, especially after the intensity of the last week. My mind needs no further burdening; Malc and I decide it is down to me, to play my game and to be free with it.

Early on, I take the game down the backhand wall where I reap great dividends with several cutting backhand drops, one of my strongest shots. It is the best start I could have imagined and he knows it as he begins to argue with the referee on the last point of the game, which I win to take the opener.

Physically I seem to be in good fettle, and feel strong in the early exchanges of the second. We go toe-to-toe up until the midway point. Ever so slowly he begins to open the court, asking me to move a little further each time. We start the third at parity. Despite a significant injection of pace from him at the end of the second my tank feels nowhere near empty. Malc asks for more before we lock horns in the third. He is delighted with what I am doing on there and feels that if I can recreate a spell of play like the first, I am back in contention. He asks for due attention when taking Nick wide on the cross court, especially from left to right.

Nick begins to find ways of moving me more and more and midway through the third, his ears are pricking, my body dwindling. Suddenly it occurs to me that I simply might not have enough in me to win this final. He draws away comprehensively, 11-2. Malc knows exhaustion is setting in, and he doesn't need to hear it from me. He understands what has been involved this week and the toll it has taken. After the third, he tells me to maintain the effort, however tired, and plies me with positive feedback about how well I have done.

Despite some tenacity on my part, Nick drags me around the court in the fourth and it is a formality, 11-3. I have given everything but Nick is the best player in the world, deserving of the title. I race outside and keel over on a grass verge 100 metres away from the court. An outpouring of emotion takes place in which I scream, bang my hands and racket in to the floor, and throw my bandanna and wristband in to the sea, not through disappointment or sadness; no, this is more of a release of the emotion and intensity that has built up over the last ten days. I have given my best and couldn't have won tonight. Malc lays a hand on my shoulder. Time to gather myself for the presentation ceremony.

I accept the runner-up trophy once again, and watch Nick receive the keys to a brand new Volkswagen. Pity. I quite fancied that car.

Then comes the hard part, that low time after big matches which I keep mentioning is so draining. Malc, staying in my room, drifts off to sleep. I watch television, unable to rid myself of thoughts of the final. This is a good night, too, where I have no regrets, made no mistakes and know that I have given the best account of myself possible. Still I lie awake, adrenalin flying through my body, unable to relinquish the intensity of the night, the week. I accept that there is little chance of sleep, especially as a 5am wake up call beckons for an 8am flight. Restless, I snatch a couple of 15 minutes' spells of sleep, if only because of exhaustion.

11 December 2010

Getting to the airport for our next port of call – New Delhi – was hard work. Cameron Pilley, one of the leading Aussie players travelling with us in the car, had passport problems and it seemed to take hours to get there. Berating him for having had the misfortune to be an Australian, we threatened to leave him. Worse was to come: at check-in Mick was told that his visa was not valid for India; it transpired that he had bought a double entry visa just before the Commonwealth Games, but some small print stated that he could not make the second visit until two months had passed. Two months had not passed. A ridiculous restriction.

Mick was now faced with the following options: stay in Bahrain (at least he could get a drink, unlike dry Saudi) and wait for the consulate to open, where he could attempt to obtain a visa, fly home, or use his charm to worm his way on to the plane. He is always telling me to keep my glass half-full, but now his own levels of positivity would be greatly tested by this unfortunate mishap.

So we left, telling him we were glad to see the back of him in an attempt to lighten the mood. It certainly looked bleak and the desk attendant was unable to cut him any slack. It appeared that poor Mick, not having touched alcohol for ten days (a minor miracle for him), was in a dire situation. Now stuck in Bahrain, the man who makes 'everything happen' would be tested to the limit if he was to get to Delhi at all. And he was on his own.

Malc and I sipped coffee and boarded the plane. I sent a few texts to Mick asking if he had got anywhere but only received vague responses. As Malc settled in to his window seat and I shifted hand luggage into the overhead cabin, having accepted this depressing eventuality, I glanced to the front of the plane, and in all his leather-cladded glory, there he was, my manager. I clapped eyes on him and did a double take, wondering how he had possibly managed to get on the plane. I fisted the air at him, the World Open final already far from my mind. Malc couldn't believe it when I told him Mick was walking towards us.

We all sat together, suddenly feeling elated. Malcolm and I pretended to be disappointed but we were secretly delighted. Mick had avoided the claws of control, but still had to actually get in to India. The Indians do corruption better than anyone so we felt that we were in a healthy position. We asked him how he had done it and I don't think he really knew. Perhaps his lack of irascibility and ability to remain positive helped him with the officials.

It was at this point, after being perilously close to a minor disaster, that we saw the funny side. We talked and laughed for three hours, and it is at times like these that life is at its very best. To make things even better, the air hostess, at the beginning of the flight, passed by us. 'Excuse me', Mick says. 'Do you serve alcohol, darlin'? He somehow manages to say 'darlin' without it being patronising. She was a woman with a sense of humour who gave as good as she got, replying: 'Yes, darling! Of course we do!' Mick was made up. The wind had changed. We all had a drink: a wine for Malc, a vodka for myself, and about eight cans of Heineken for Mick.

At passport control we started sweating again, knowing that Mick wasn't completely out of the woods. I stood in one queue, Mick and Malc in another. Malc went first and impressed the passport control officer with the fact that he is coach to the Indian No 1 squash player, mentioning the Commonwealths and the Asian Games, huge events in

India.   Mick followed directly behind stating, in what turned out to be a perfectly executed operation, that he is the Indian No 1's manager. After that display the officer could do little else but let him through. We arrived in India happy.

NINE

THE HIGHS AND THE LOWS

15 December 2010

Delhi is the last tournament of the year. Getting up to play again at the highest level three days after a World Open final is a seriously tough proposition. I, like others I'm sure, am flagging and have had nowhere near enough time to refresh.

Ali Anwar Reda, the Egyptian player I played in the first round, was fresh and I knew how tough it would be, such is the strength of these players. It was one of the hardest matches of the two weeks. After one of my greatest achievements in Saudi one might think that I was near untouchable and replete with confidence. Anything but, I'm afraid. Lacking just about every attribute needed to play squash well – speed, stamina, agility, mental assuredness – I bumbled through the match feeling as fragile as a ever. The only thing that saved me was my experience. I have been through this many times now and I know how to deal with it.

One of the worst examples of this was at the World Junior Championships in India. The very morning after I had won the world under-19 individual final, realising a dream I had held since I was a little boy, David, who was in charge of the junior team, selected me to play in our first group match against Ireland. I had lost about forty points in the whole individual event and yet I found myself standing at 9-9 in the fourth with the Irish No 1. David sternly asked me to concentrate for five-minute spells at a time, and in what must be our only ever argument, I petulantly stormed off saying, 'I will win, but just let me do it in my own way. There's no way I can concentrate, so let me continue to make a pig's ear of it'.

It is not that a heavy schedule and such a high as last week brings on any lack of motivation, but that the mind and body simply cannot repeat the standard so soon. Last week's buzz was so elevated and its demands so draining, so intense, that the body goes into some sort of shut down mode.

It is striking how different the feeling is now, after four months of brutal squash and travel , compared to the feeling I had as I embarked on the new season back in early August. Back then, hardened from severe training, I could have run through walls. Now, held together by tapes, painkillers and Malc, Mick and David, who are here with me, I can barely run.

I tell myself it isn't that bad and that every other player must feel the same. The other trick is to make sure all of this junk doesn't come across on court.

I learnt a very valuable lesson back in 2009 regarding this phenomenon of body language. I had just been beaten by Nick in that awful British Open final and five days later, angry, depressed, blistered and exhausted, I found myself at Heathrow, in preparation for the Petrosport tournament in Cairo. Unsettled by personal issues and devastated by my second near miss in the British Open, I was ready for meltdown in the security queue. I had never come closer to turning back home to Leeds than this. I didn't want to see any of the players, and I didn't want to play squash.

For the three days before the event, practice was out of the question and I spent long hours in the hotel room alone. I saw nothing and no one for days. Even if I had the physical capability to work, there was a severe lack of motivation.

I went two down in no time to Farhan Mehboob in the first round and didn't even think about winning, in fact I didn't really want to win. I wanted to be at home with Vanessa, whose loyalty and care was steadfast, unlike everything else at that time it seemed. Although nonplussed about the outcome, I had travelled a long way, and however bad the situation was I have been brought up to give my very best at all times. For this reason I never stopped trying. He made errors and suddenly I had won the match 3-2.

I thought it was a bonus, a few more ranking points to my name for getting to the second round. I had Peter Barker next, and knew I had little chance but would again try. As expected he won the first well and led in the second, holding game balls. I kept trying.

I sat down in between games and couldn't believe we were level at 1-1. Back on in the third, I went 7-1 up. What is happening here? Another rally or two and he offered me his hand, conceding the match. Talk about a get out of jail card.

Twenty four hours later I lost 3-2 to Ramy in a close encounter, and wasn't far off reaching the semis. It proved to me that I had been right to keep trying, and to keep holding my head up. While I was thinking everything was going against me, I hadn't realised that things weren't running that kindly for the others either. Peter had a nasty blister, and it came down to which of us was the last man standing.

18 December 2010

I have reached my second major final in a week, after beating Hisham Ashour. Whatever happens, I have to be happy with my achievements during this period. Once again I face Nick and I have to wonder how many other sports have featured two Englishmen in so many finals.

This year we've contested the National, Swedish, Commonwealth, World and now the Punj Lloyd Masters finals, along with the Canary Wharf, Virginia, and Australian semis.

When I woke up, I knew I was not going to be able to break my losing run against him. I felt absolutely awful and couldn't eat breakfast. I was a finalist in the second biggest tournament on the tour, though. It was decent consolation.

Because of the volume of squash over the past months, and with the onset of complete lethargy, there was no way I could tire my brain and body further by concentrating or thinking about the match, and so I didn't. I read an excerpt from Michael Johnson's autobiography recently, which said that he didn't spend much time visualising and mentally rehearsing his performances. He figured that all his work had been done before hand and that there was little point in wasting any further energy.

This led me to surmise that, especially as I was under the weather, I was best off lying about in bed watching period dramas. So that's what I did, skipping practice. I was capable of little else. I didn't let on to anyone, not even Dad or Mick, but I was holding on by the skin of my teeth. My body has coped as well as I could ever have hoped, playing so many matches, but I knew it couldn't go on for much longer, and every mental build up to every match, each new warm-up, every mental push at 7-7 is taking its toll now.

After a bit of lunch I lay on the bed for a while, then gathered my kit and downed some paracetamol and ibuprofen. Starting to feel better, I headed off in a car that had been arranged for Nick and myself. It is unusual for us to talk before matches, but we spoke about the complete lack of publicity both of us have had after contesting the first World Open final between English players last week. I have had no response from the media whatsoever, and Nick said he had done one interview.

We arrived at the Commonwealth Games squash centre, which has been in a state of disuse since the Games ended. Starting the warm-up I knew something wasn't right. I felt better than I did in the morning, but felt full and bloated, my stomach seemingly unable to digest the little food I had eaten. After the match Malcolm said he knew there was something the matter as he watched my warm-up, although nothing was mentioned by either of us at the time.

I suppose in many respects this was not the match with which to end a very good year. I tried hard but was dragged from pillar to post. I petulantly snapped at Malc inbetween the second and third and made a gesture to the crowd when I thought that their shouting implied I could do better. It was unsatisfactory but we addressed it afterwards and spoke in depth. I apologised and he said although he completely understood my frustrations after all the travel and play, the display didn't suit me and the gestures to the crowd didn't look right.

Flashback
31 August 2006

The eve of the World Open in Cairo. My eyes open to a black room and before I can think of anything I am left breathless by an excruciating feeling in my stomach. I breathe heavily, forced into an unfamiliar hyperventilation. I am only slightly aware of the unrelenting city traffic below my window – because it is the middle of the night and this level of noise would be unusual anywhere else – and of the flashing lights of the cars which are visible through a small chink of unclosed curtain in the corner. I flick the light switch and an extraordinary surge of pain comes over me.

I stumble to the bathroom and puke and soil myself in the most undignified manner. Thank God I am in a room alone, and not sharing with another player - had it been any other tournament then in all likelihood my unlucky room mate would have been woken by the noise – perfect preparation the night before a match. After this initial phase, I keel over on the bathroom floor and wonder if Anthony Ricketts, who took a room a couple of doors down from me, has heard me, so loud and violent are my expulsions.

I have no idea what to do as this situation is entirely new. I somehow manage to make it down to the reception and tell them in no uncertain terms that I need to see a doctor immediately. Both receptionists look at me blankly, then 'um' and 'agh' until I start crying in front of them. I ring Dad, who is in his own room, and am so grateful for his presence. Waiting for him to come to reception, I stagger to the toilet, stooping like an old man, drawing looks from one or two players and other hotel guests.

I exit in extreme pain to find Malc turning the corner looking worried. He manages to pin down a doctor and then escorts me upstairs, propping me up, acting as a crutch. I have no energy or ability to tell him what is going on. My distress is evident, which doesn't help his frame of mind.

There are two beds in his room so I lie on one and by this stage the next bout of vomiting is imminent. This continues for the next few hours, in intervals of about 25 minutes. Malc, now beside himself, tries to follow me in but I say that this bit is for my eyes only, for his sake if nothing else. I retch from the very bottom of my being. Malc comes into the bathroom and is shocked at what he sees.

After cleaning up, he settles on his own bed, in the hope

that we will both sleep. At this stage the doctor arrives and administers some pills. I get the feeling something is horribly wrong here and it needs more than paracetamol. Ritwik Bhattachyra, a fellow player, who had heard about the problem has given me some rehydration salts to sip, a gesture which does me little good but which later I will come to appreciate. After a little fluid and a doze, I am ready to puke again. I switch the light on, amble to the bathroom, and repeat the whole undignified process. As anticipated, the pills do nothing and come up with whatever food is now left in my stomach. Such is the feeling of mental and physical debilitation during this cyclical process that it feels as though every bodily organ in my depleted body is being wrenched from its moorings.

I know my system is being put upon in a way that it never has before. A hospital stay in Cairo at 2:30am might be the answer. 'Hospital? How will that work?' Malc asks.

'I don't know. I want to die.' And I really did. I nod off until the next wave hits me. 'I need to do it again.' The respite is all too transient. This time I hear a touch of incredulous frustration in Malc's voice. 'Again? My God.'

'I desperately need to drink', I wail. 'But my body won't let me. I need to go to hospital now. I need to go. I just know'.

During these hellish few hours, Malc is unbelievable. Apart from doing everything I ask of him, he takes on the unpleasant job of cleaning up after me as only a parent can, thereby sparing the maid the most unholy task the following morning. I don't think he can quite believe that he is on the verge of hailing a cab to a Cairo hospital.

In the cab, I sprawl on his lap in the back seat. I am only faintly aware of his instructions to the driver, and the next thing I know I am being wheeled to a waiting area where two Egyptian receptionists with limited English lay me on a bed. I vehemently exclaim that I need to be put on a drip. Malcolm repeats my calls in a deeper, more authoritative voice, overpowering my faint pleas, until they give in. Once they understand, an absurd scenario ensues during which the two men ask for payment in advance. They require a credit card but Malc only has cash, and too little. As is his way, he proceeds to fly off into a tirade about people not accepting cash any more and how stupid the world has become.

'He is writhing about on the floor; he needs to go in immediately,' he says. 'We will pay the money later. Come on!'

I am in a wheelchair and for the first time I wonder what the hell we are doing here. I'm decrepit and utterly useless, and Malc is bellowing at confused Arabs the night before the biggest squash tournament of the year, for which I had prepared so hard.

It transpires that I have my own credit cards with me, God only knows how, and Malc supplies them with one. One way or another I sign it to make the payment and as I sit there, delicate and infirm, signing a receipt in desperation, this is as bad and as strange as it gets.

I am wheeled to my own private room, where nurses put me on a bed, and it is not long before the drip is in my arm. In my eyes the needle is a magic wand. Malc sits there looking worried and when I awaken after another disturbed doze, he asks me questions, answers to which I haven't the strength to give. 'Dad, just go. It's no use. They'll look after me now. Get some sleep.'

I don't know what was in the drip, but for the next 36 hours I sleep a lot, waking up regularly to feel the agonising throbbing of my insides. Malc flits in and out of the hospital and tries to be of help. I spend most of my time doubled up, in the foetal position. I am still unable to hold any type of conversation, and vaguely recall Malc telling me that he has officially pulled me out of the event; it doesn't really need saying.

My mate Ricketts comes along for half an hour, during which time I groaned and dozed, unable to talk. We knew each other well enough not to worry about making small talk.

2 September 2006

I wake and am immediately struck by a feeling of extreme elation. For the first time, the edge has been taken off the pain. I still feel weak and ill, but I am a hundred times improved. I almost laugh with sheer happiness that the pain has eased. Of all the great and gratifying sensations in our lives, whether it be eating when hungry, or drinking when thirsty, this surpasses them all. It is often said that the pleasure doesn't feel half as good without the preceding pain, and there is nothing truer. To have delved to the very depths and been in such a state – and it is far from over I know that – I now fully understand the sheer joy of simply feeling 'OK', which under normal circumstances I take for granted every day.

Not long after, I receive a call from Malc and he hears the music in my voice, immediately recognising a changed tone, which thrills and relieves him all at once. We conduct a buoyant conversation, and I know we can relax a little for the first time in nearing 48 hours. I spend a little time replying to text messages, and reading, before having my first proper meeting with the Cairo doctor.

'I told you some things when I last visited. You may not have understood everything. You were sedated,' he reveals gently with a smile which I am now happy to reciprocate. 'You look better. You have had acute gastroenteritis. It may have been a type of food poisoning such as salmonella, but we couldn't get a stool sample from you – you were in such a bad state so we won't know. Now, do you feel hungry at all?' I certainly don't, and won't for days, but so thrilled and elated am I to not feel the appalling pain any longer that food is barely even a thought. I am happy enough to feel the pure heaven of relative comfort.

During those first hours with the edge taken off the pain, my mind takes me back a few weeks earlier to a long conversation I had on the phone with Damon in which we covered all the possible pitfalls regarding food in Egypt. I always erred on the side of caution when in India, Pakistan and Egypt and in the past had been extremely careful. I remember Damon explicitly telling me to avoid buffet food and that paired with my own ingrained paranoia makes me realise that I should have known better.

He told me to always eat freshly prepared food, and I had even written it on a sheet of paper which I brought to Cairo with me; it now lay useless in my bag in the hotel room. After the first couple of nights eating the buffet and feeling okay I became complacent, and as our meals were included in the tournament deal, I almost felt I should eat it. That was my mistake. I erroneously assumed that having had no ill effects early on, I could keep eating the same things. As I come to my senses in the bleak hospital room, I realise how stupid I have been, to seek advice and then go on to completely dismiss it just for the sake of convenience. After all the hard work I put in over the summer, I begin to understand that this carelessness will put my whole season in jeopardy. It is a grave mistake on my part rather than an unlucky accident.

20 December 2010

I have been looking forward to this day for weeks now, a day which promised a certain release of tension, where I might drink beer and eat cake, but it seems to be falling a bit flat. Our flight is cancelled because of snow, and I feel hungover without having had any alcohol last night. Mick is dying for me to get on the liquor with him but I haven't got it in me to contemplate the stuff.

So we sit in the lobby and shamelessly slag each other off, whilst organising alternative flights. It is difficult to quite know what the Indian waitresses make of it all, but they smile all the same. With no matches to play, no coaching to attend, and no meetings to sit through, this is our time. Soon, I give in and the wine is ordered.

At the airport, Mick downs some more wine and as we board the plane in Zurich, after a testing overnighter from Delhi, bleary eyed, I hear Mick order again. It is officially 8am. He is undeterred, on a mission. It is Christmas, after all. We both gang up on Malc because he keeps pretending to refuse to spend Christmas Day with Vanessa and I in Leeds, saying he would rather be alone. We all know he is joking, but we give him grief all the same for being eccentric.

Finally back home, I am relieved to have missed the BBC's Sports Personality of the Year Awards. Unfortunately, half of today's existing sports don't even get mentioned. And yes I find it sad that Andy Murray, Britain's lone tennis player, can be a major contender when English Squash can boast the world's No 1 and world champion, the two world championship finalists and the women's world No 2. Not one of England's most famous and respected sportsmen have ever achieved what Nick has achieved in 2010. Wayne Rooney hasn't come close to being the equivalent of a world champion or world No 1, neither has the ultimate sporting idol in this country, David Beckham. Just a mention of Nick would have been a start. What a gross injustice it is that English squash players, rowers, tri-athletes and divers – amongst the best athletes in the world – are so far down the pecking order in terms of recognition.

24 December 2010

On the way to the squash club to watch the kid's nativity play, I stopped in town, not to do Christmas shopping but to buy four chocolate mousses. I planned to have two but ended up eating them all in the car, one after the other.

Had a relaxing evening watching the kids and meeting up with one or two people at the club, until Chinny, a long-term member and close mate of Mick's came up to me, drunk, and declared that I needed to eat 'a bit of meat' if I wanted to beat Nick Matthew.

You can imagine my reaction. People lose sight of an achievement if it is not a win. To reach two major finals in three weeks is special, but as usual our critical society sees the negative side of it – two more losses to Nick. I tell Chinny to take a second and ask himself how preposterous this sounds. What could it possibly be that makes meat so magical and performance enhancing? I really nail in to him, pretending to be far more upset than I actually am.

I advise him to play around with a search engine and do some research before he comes out with any more nonsense.

25 December 2010

Vanessa and I make Christmas dinner and Malc does eventually agree to stay over. We watch *Oliver*, just the three of us. Life probably doesn't get much better than this: not because it is Christmas, but because I never get to spend time with my two closest pals and watch my favourite TV, and eat all my favourite foods in chosen quantities.

And yes, it goes without saying: no training. Even squash players take Christmas day off.

TEN

THE CHEEK OF IT

4 January 2011

Went to Chapel Allerton in Leeds for a solo practice this morning, before having the afternoon off. On the adjacent court was a young chap, late twenties, practising by himself for quite long periods. At one stage our rest time coincided, and we began chatting. A few of the obvious questions surfaced: how often do you practice? Where do you train? I asked him about doing solo on a Tuesday afternoon, and said I was impressed with his dedication. I could sense him wanting to ask for a knock.

At the end of the conversation, as I returned to do some more practice, he said awkwardly: 'Well if you ever fancy a game let me know', and with that I was back on court, snarling.

If I ever fancied a game? I am a professional, it is my job. I do it all the time. I always fancy a game. It is what I do. I could think of nothing better than to stay on for an extra 20 minutes of my day off and play someone I have never met. Perhaps I am wrong but people have no shame. If I had the time, there are about a hundred kids at Pontefract who deserve it before a person like this, but these kids, whom I know well, never ask. Perhaps these people think we hang around squash clubs all day offering games to people.

I get regular proposals and requests for favours. The other day at Pontefract, a member well known to me but not particularly close stopped me.

'Oh James, I was going to ask you, have you got any rackets to sell?'

'No, but there are some in the shop upstairs, or you

can buy them on several good websites. I don't sell rackets.'

'Can you not get a deal? Reduced price?'

'Erm no.' I thought about saying that I'll see what I can do, but didn't even bother with that. Some people seem to forget that we are squash players, not salesmen.

The best example in recent times was in Boulder at the Colorado training camp. I was lifting weights in the gym, when a fresh-faced American club member, quite full of himself, came up to me, in the middle of my session I might add, and said: 'Hey Willstrop, you wanna hit some balls with me?'

Incensed , I responded petulantly, hoping to make the bloke feel smaller than a pea:

'Willstrop?' I winced. 'I'll come on court with you if you pay me $5000. Otherwise, it really isn't worth my while.'

With that I turned my back and devoured my next set of squats.

6 January 2011

A new year and new developments within England Squash and Racketball. We had a meeting with performance director Keir Worth, in which we discussed the developments regarding coaching roles at the association. Jenny Duncalf, Peter Barker and Nick were present, and I think we were keen to understand fully, as the leading players on the programme, how decisions had been made of late, bearing in mind the extent of the personnel changes.

Over the course of the meeting talk soon centred on the future of English squash, or rather the state of junior squash in this country. I was the only member of the group who spoke of it remotely positively. The apparently poor standard is one of the reasons the association are keen to make these changes.

We need to be very careful when looking at the British Junior Open results (the most prestigious junior tournament in the world). On the surface England is sparsely represented; there are perhaps a few English quarter-finalists, a couple of semi-finalists and maybe one finalist. It's not setting the world on fire and the English are not dominating the whole scene as the Egyptians seem to be able to do, but historically English juniors have never won across the board in this way.

At this year's British Junior Open, which finished only today in Sheffield, England had 10 quarter-finalists in all age groups, two of whom reached the semis, and Emily Whitlock won the under-17 final, the first home grown British Junior Open Champion since 2002.

The best junior players in this country therefore are knocking on the door, which is good enough if senior success is the eventual target. These players have plenty of time for learning and improving to achieve their world class potential.

The two countries, England and Egypt, are chalk and cheese in terms of their methods and development of their players. This tournament acts as a smokescreen, deceiving everyone into believing that our kids are of a poor standard just because they aren't cleaning up or at least competing with the Egyptians.

Egyptian juniors are ensconced in a focused grooming system which is hell bent on producing prodigies from as early an age as possible. Indeed, in Alexandria a centre of excellence with up to 30 courts is due to start blooding the next batch of winners in the next few years. A scary thought. English juniors are brought up more slowly; they play other sports, do their school work and are exposed to many other activities in their younger years, not necessarily concentrating on one specifically. They may initially be behind their Arab counterparts because of this.

Perhaps this is why the English often find the power and energy to peak and be successful later in their careers. I also believe they are at a physical disadvantage as juniors. Egyptians and Pakistanis seem inherently stronger at a young age.

This is a side point – and everyone in squash knows it – but certain Eastern countries are known for disclosing false ages on entry forms or passports, effectively cheating their age, making it harder still for westerners who cannot employ such corruption.

Nick is the perfect example of a late developer, only ever winning one British title in his junior career, but completely surpassing those achievements a decade later as a senior. When I won the British Junior Open in 1997, the only English winner, people were saying the same negative things of English squash then. Now look at that generation of English squash players 13 years on. From being reasonable in the junior ranks in 1997, that same generation of players has become arguably the strongest English senior squad ever.

It would be easy to expect more of the same from the England seniors of tomorrow, but this is a dangerous assumption; this era might never again be emulated, let alone by the next generation. Due to the cyclical nature of sport it is impossible to expect nations with strong reputations in certain sports to continue to be world beaters. Take the Australian cricket team, or the Khan squash dynasty from Pakistan. Both nations in their corresponding sports have suffered weak spells from time to time, and at the time of writing both are enduring slumps.

However good Egypt or England are in squash presently, they weren't always this good in the past and probably won't always be this good in the future.

England Squash have funded and supported their best players brilliantly, and this support has produced results, most notably in the senior ranks. I know I couldn't have been as successful without the funding and support that is provided through the English Institute of Sport. I hope our governing body continues to have faith in the system they have built, which at present is the best in the world.

Back on court and I'm consulting the physio about my knee – it is creaky and not entirely pain free and I'm going to have to keep an eye on the volume of squash that is imminent. Obliterated by the schedule in the autumn months, I am not sure I have quite had enough time over Christmas to regroup.

ELEVEN

BACK IN TOO SOON

12 January 2011

The World Series Finals in London is an exciting event, with the top eight players on show. I just hope it hasn't arrived a little too soon. The set up at the Queen's Club really is slick. A large tent-like bubble structure houses the glass court and it is as special a squash arena as I have ever seen. The brand new court is purple and pristine, almost revolutionary, with cat's eyes delineating the nick between the side wall and the floor. Ziad has thrown everything at the event and it looks as if the week will see the PSA, the men's world tour, invite potential sponsors and partners to show that this sport can deliver.

Despite warming down well, having treatment last night and only playing two games of squash, my back is in pieces. After three weeks of not playing a game, it is shocked by what I asked of it in my opening match against Alister Walker. Ali played well and we had a good, clean scrap in the first, a real blow out for the lungs. Athletes often talk about match fitness, as if it is different to ordinary fitness. It is a fascinating phenomenon about which I was talking to Mark Campbell only the other day. He claimed that his athletes can be as fit as ever, in peak condition, yet their first foray into proper competition after a spell of absence can often leave them flagging in no time. In most sports, supreme general fitness can only take an athlete so far, and if they lack significant match play there is a tendency to come up short.

During the season the challenge is to maintain a healthy balance between matchplay and training. Overdo the matchplay and mental freshness, strength and fitness is compromised. Overdo the training and a player can be super fit but lose some of the specific sharpness, guile and know-how that comes with competitive matches. Sometimes the difficulty in obtaining this balance over a season stems from all the travel, which is often a damaging factor.

It may be surprising that it doesn't take long for a squash player to find himself a little rusty. How often has it been said by the top players that it was 'good to get that one out of the way' when referring to first-round matches in tournaments? There are several reasons why the best players are cautious and come a little unstuck in early rounds: often the first match comes after a break in tournaments. It is the one in which the top seeds are likely to be rusty. Additionally, the first round opponents are often qualifiers who come into the event having played a couple of games. With nothing to lose and having the added motivation that there is little pressure on them, they often perform well enough to cause problems.

My body will feel even worse after just having played three intense games against Ramy. He himself is recovering from injury and is therefore not in the best shape mentally. It would be fair to say he is not in world-beating form. Nevertheless, he managed to make me look average in the first but I responded well and won.

Shabana and Nick played a game of high quality. I watched with some of the other players in the warm-up room and we were having a great time. Shabana was keen and fit, tantalising with his trademark dives, giving the crowd something to really cheer about, and the third game ended 17-15 in his favour.

13 Janary 2011

For the first time in my World Series Finals' history, I found myself in a good position, having won two games out of two, and in the semi-finals. I felt as if I had almost done enough, and was in danger of being lulled into a false sense of security. I had to beat Thierry tonight, who is always dangerous.

Ramy and I had flown around the court and the pace was exacting; Thierry, on the other hand, teased with his patted straight lengths, and the more I forced the issue in an inelegant attempt to expose the niggle that he has been carrying all week, the more it felt as if I was treading water. I scraped the first in a tie-breaker, which was all I needed to go through to the semis, and then took a good lead in the second, before he came back at me at the end. I jarred my ankle quite badly again which put me in an awful mood. I didn't want to have to go into another match against Nick with body issues.

14 January 2011

I was convincingly beaten again by Nick, 11-4, 11-6, 11-8 in 46 minutes – 12 or so times in a row now. Others seem to be more bothered about it than I am. I am able to take it in my stride and accept that he is a man in the prime of his sporting life. Sometimes you have to take your hat off to that person at such a time. Meanwhile, I have to be diligent and focused on changing the status quo.

Sadly, the defeat was one of the most dissatisfying nights of my career. I didn't want to push, having neither the mental or physical capacity to deal with what he was doing. To be lining up to play Nick so soon after the bruising encounters before Christmas was something with which I was incapable of coping. A burned out candle, all I wanted was to be off court, and it was the supporters from Pontefract and my friends, Vanessa, Malc and Mick, whose presence made me eke out a performance.

I lost the first convincingly and stormed to the back behind the doors, crouching on the floor, feeling almost on the verge of a breakdown. Malcolm was concerned and slightly confused, asking what the problems were. 'I'm at the end here', I said. 'I can't do any more.'

I played out the match as best I could but there was little hope. I had a microphone placed in my face immediately afterwards and I was never going to be giving off pleasantries. I was honest and pessimistic; anything remotely positive at that moment would have been false.

Malc was dejected but supportive afterwards and, after so many losses against Nick, it becomes harder to blank out the doubts altogether. It's only natural. I know that when I can get myself in the best shape possible, and after some improvement, something which is so difficult at present when all I do is play, I can get there.

15 January 2011

I entered the gates at the Queen's Club to see crowds of people on the steps near the clubhouse which seemed peculiar. The tournament organisers said that the final was in great danger of not going ahead because of problems within the structure of the marquee which housed the court, an apparent consequence of the high winds.

After much to-ing and fro-ing, it was formally announced that the final, between Nick Matthew and Amr Shabana, would not be played. All other possibilities were looked into. Could they play on the club courts? Would it be feasible to come back tomorrow? Could it be played elsewhere in London, somewhere that could cope with a sizeable crowd? In the end the answer to all of these questions was no, and the match was postponed indefinitely until further notice. A shame.

Not long afterwards, the most bizarre scenes unfolded and the whole club was entirely evacuated; the fire brigade appeared on the lawns. Apparently the inflatable bubble structure was deemed dangerous enough that it might explode. It sounded implausible but that was the message. It had all happened incredibly quickly and was surely the most bizarre end to a major event I had ever witnessed.

Not only that, but how ironic, sad and unjust it seemed for Ziad, whose efforts for this event had been greater and more clinically formulated than ever before. Neither he, nor the sport deserved this.

17 January 2011

Stayed in London over the weekend ready for a flight to New York and the defence of my title at the Tournament of Champions. It's exciting to be going back to the Big Apple and I can't wait to get to JFK, that gateway to the free world where burly security types scream and shout at everyone to get in line and do this and do that.

TWELVE

NEW YORK, NEW YORK

18 January 2011

Went to see a play called *Lombardi*, about a legendary American Football coach. Despite having much of its dialogue peppered with talk of gridiron, it was excellent. We were lucky enough to witness a question and answer session afterwards by the director and actors which made the evening doubly fascinating. At squash exhibitions we often end with a short session of crowd interaction, and I have now realised why: it made the stars of the show more tangible, and the topics were fascinating to boot. For an audience member, such an end to the evening was hugely enjoyable.

The following night saw the World Squash Awards take place. It was perhaps unsurprising that the awards, held in the US for the first time, had been Americanised, in what was presumably a necessary measure in order to fund the event. We found ourselves enduring an American take on proceedings, so much so that the ceremony should have been retitled: the ' US squash and hardball awards'.

Squash in the States is still elitist and inaccessible to the so called working classes. Clubs exist at the top of tall business buildings in the big cities and people on the streets have little chance of finding the game. This has changed recently because of institutions such as StreetSquash, which has successfully brought it to the less fortunate.

The rich who play the sport encourage their kids to play so that they may have a path to a good college if they don't succeed in other areas. Very few, decent junior players ever even think about turning professional and conducting a squash career whilst attending university; to compete at the very top of the world game having studied extensively in America is a near impossibility.

It is noticeable that Americans like to make their mark on everything. They have sports, gridiron and baseball, which are played by few other nations, yet whose competitions are named 'World Series'.

In squash, Americans have even invented their own terminology, calling 'drives' 'rails' and 'counter drops' 're-drops', and recently certain US authorities have attempted to tinker with the rules, advocating the exclusion of 'let calls' in squash altogether.

So it is no surprise that the awards were given gratuitously to American people, who are not of a world standard in squash, at a *world* ceremony. If the awards had been hosted in Kuwait, would the awards have been distributed to Kuwaiti squash players, who are not strong in the sport?

A US coach recently wrote a book about his successes with a college team. Americans see college squash as *the* standard. It is their pinnacle. If you were to ask the world's top twenty squash players, they would be unable to name one of the players in this team – Trinity – the most famous college sports team in the USA. This doesn't seem to stop the book being of interest here, and it will probably sell more copies than this one.

The organisers have done a brilliant job staging the World Squash Awards each year and their prerogative was to make sure the event happened at all; undoubtedly its staging demands considerable expense. Hosting the ceremony in New York surely helped that and having said all this, adding the American slant was probably unavoidable.

I realise I have written less than generously of Americans. Before the law suits come in, I have merely made honest generalisations. Their cities are some of the most exciting the world over and I can unequivocally say the Tournament of Champions crowd is the best of all audiences to play in front of. US squash has staged some incredible events over the years, and an exciting three year run of the US Open looks to be in place in Philadelphia.

For me, it only seemed a short time ago since I walked through the famous station to play my matches during that dream run last January. So soon and I was back again. I opened up with a win over the dangerous Jonathan Kemp, whose pace and variation can be troubling, before beating Spain's Borja Golan, who came back from nine months out injured in the summer. My play was fluent and crisp but it won't be long before Borja is back amongst it. He has a good attitude.

I adapted my game well enough in the next round to beat Mohamed El Shorbagy, the young Egyptian who is now knocking on the door of the top eight with his fast-paced attacking style. I've withstood his strengths well in the last few matches we have played and feel I have established some control over him, though they have been intense and have demanded full concentration.

Peter Nicol, who is used to winning here, has been helping me this week and his advice has been simple and effective. I always find that the best coaches can simplify matters sufficiently; there is nothing worse than being told 10 things in the space of a two minute gap in between games.

I was off in three games; my body is pleased and so is my mind. They are serving me well, and I am rewarded with 48 hours rest – two of which are spent watching *Mary Poppins* at the New Amsterdam Theatre with Mick and Vanessa – to get ready for another semi-final in the Beaux-

Arts Vanderbilt Hall with Ramy, who beat a gallant David Palmer.

26 January 2011

Almost a year to the day and I repeat many of the rituals and pre-match routines to be employed against the same player in the same building, only in a different round. Walking through Grand Central for the ninth year, there is an impulse to recall last January's performance which will stand out as one of the most special. Media and fans have been asking what it means to be the defending champion and whether it is helping. I've never been one for overstating it, but I can't help but remember with affection what happened last year.

Nevertheless I respond guardedly, insisting that there are several quality players who want to stop me successfully defending the title, and the fairytale could easily be prevented. My mood is more relaxed here than at this stage last year, now that I'm learning to lighten up around matches. Before, I was a bag of nerves during the build-up, every little move given great significance. Age and experience seem to have taught my brain to understand that the intense work has been done before match days, and that to let go a little come the big matches can help a lot. Now I do things I didn't used to, things that are enjoyable, that help to maintain a relaxed frame of mind. Over-intensity and over-analysis are often the key factors in stifling sporting excellence.

After last week's exhausted performance in London, lacking the will to even play, I am renewed and revitalised, and have reason to think I'm in as good a shape as Ramy. He hasn't had the greatest few weeks, most of it spent in Yorkshire seeing the physio, where he has undergone a period of education on injuries and their prevention through rehab. Because of a lack of knowledge in this area in Egypt (their attention to detail on the physical side of things seems to be seriously lacking), I gather he is learning a thing or two. Amr Shabana told me once that he had to look up an injury online, diagnosing and treating it himself, such was the lack of support he had in that area.

I arrive at Grand Central and pick up a double espresso, persisting with the caffeine ritual. Keeping my head down, the last thing I want to do is catch the eye of a long-lost friend, or any friend for that matter, when there is too much to be thinking about. I'm inclined to be impolite when small talk is required so it is better not to look at all.

The 'social mire', as it has been termed, is the area a player treads at his or her peril. Apart from when I play, I avoid going into it at tournaments unless I have time. These areas are full of polite conversation and small talk, which is all very nice, and being a player at a big event means that people are interested and inquisitive, for which I am appreciative. Sadly for me I am not blessed with the patience or social graces that are often expected, especially around match times.

As a counterpoint, the wonderful thing about squash is that it has retained the capacity to allow both its stars and its fans to co-exist in a single environment, something which is very unusual. The players are accessible at tournaments because the sport hasn't disappeared down the agent and sports management route just yet. It is still comfortingly down to earth in the way it taps into communities, squash clubs and real people. There is a lack of exclusivity and this is one of the best things about being an underexposed sport.

I nod at the security man at the barriers who is quite familiar to me now; he knows me by name and we share a greeting every night. He wishes me good luck and I sweep by the packed hall and retreat under the scaffolding around the back of the court.

Ramy sits still, stretching. Vanessa is around and we have a giggle at having had a mini tiff earlier. She was negative about her result, losing 3-0 to Natalie Grinham, and I was frustrated because she loses perspective and fails to cut herself slack after having been ill for much of the week.

I need to be ready to move outrageously fast, therefore I prime myself to concentrate on explosive movements as the basis of the pre-match routine so that I am ready for the onslaught. Note: this is the most difficult thing to achieve on a 15-yard slippery patch of the Grand Central marble floor delegated as the players' warm-up area, which constantly has press, security and hangers-on milling about the place. It is quite possibly the worst warm-up facility ever, but then this is Grand Central Terminus; it's a marvel how a major sporting event is staged here at all. I usually warm-up with lunging and squatting exercises, but for Ramy I am concentrating on speed. Sometimes it takes me a game to adjust to his pace so I need to be ready. He still sits, whilst I jig about sweating. Is this a new warm-up routine he is implementing? Usually his warm-ups are like dynamite. What is he doing just sitting there?

I find out soon enough. The match is an anti-climax. I'm blown off court 3-0 and he played as well as I have ever seen him play. I feel as if I came into this event with too sentimental a mindset, and that I have been hanging on to the memories of last year's win, believing that I had some kind of divine right to repeat the process. Of course I could have done it again, but it was a tough call. Life is too cut-throat for fairytales. Of all people, I should have known that, especially in this half-cooked state.

Ramy wins the tournament, beating Nick in the final, and he dedicates his win 'to all of Egypt'. Squash is revered and loved there, notably by former President Hosni Mubarak. Trouble was beginning to flare in Cairo during the tournament and an uprising was imminent.

THIRTEEN

CLINT v THE BOGEY MAN

I recently zoned in on an article singling out different top class players, past and present, for their strongest attributes, and its writer mused about the merging of each player or attribute to make the perfect squash player. Nick Matthew: 'best for hard work' category; Ramy: 'best for racket speed', Jansher Khan: 'best for movement'.

Can't argue with that. I looked down and saw my name. Excellent, nice to be mentioned. My category, my great lasting legacy? Sportsmanship. Oh. They said that about all the sporting greats, didn't they? Lucky me for getting that title.

I began to imagine coaches in future generations, saying 'right kids, let's make you a world champion. First thing's first: sportsmanship. I want you to go away and watch videos of Willstrop.'

Thinking more on the subject, great champions who epitomise fairness, good sportsmanship and inner strength are plentiful, much more so than loud-mouthed, obnoxious champions in fact. There are gaggles of sporting legends who play or played out their careers in a less demonstrative and gracious manner: think Steve Ovett, Seb Coe, Sir Steve Redgrave, Dame Kelly Holmes, Stephen Hendry, Daley Thompson, Carl Lewis, Ian Thorpe. These people don't go around beating their chests and displaying outward aggression. Quite an impressive trend; perhaps I do tread the correct path after all.

Honestly, I am pleased I have a reputation for good sportsmanship and thank my Dad forcefully for having made this a priority. In his emails to me when I am away, he will often say: 'Be strong and silent; remain detached'. I love it when Malc goes inspirational and I laugh my head off at what comes next.

I can usually see it coming. Ignoring the conventional route as always, he does not mention some of the above names for inspiration, instead he talks about Clint Eastwood. It never fails to tickle me pink. Whoever knew Malc could be such a brilliant psychologist! By mentioning the revered actor's name pre-match and by asking me to emulate his strong and silent demeanour, he articulates something that just seems to resonate with me. I stay relaxed because of it.

Perhaps next time I'm at 9-9 in the fifth of a British Open final I could take it one step further: standing stock still I could ask my opponent: 'Do ya feel lucky, punk? Well, do ya?'

I may not be the hippest squash player out there, but I am pleased with the Clint Eastwood facade Malc thinks I present. The strong and silent method is the best way forward, certainly in my case. I get the usual comments: 'You are too nice, be more aggressive, be more passionate', but I can't be bothered to listen. Roger Federer is the most level-headed sportsman, giving little away, staying silent and composed like old Clint in his Westerns, and it would be foolish to question any lack of passion on the part of someone who has won multiple major tennis titles.

I wouldn't call Ramy the strong and silent type, more like the 'strong and frenetic' type, but he is respected and absolutely fair at all times. Honesty and good sportsmanship, in my opinion, are imperative in sport, for so many reasons. There is no need for deference towards opponents; outward aggression and 'in your face' passion can be a wonderful thing to watch in sport, but there is no reason why such athletes can't be fair at the same time. A steady erosion of standards threatens some sports, but on the whole most remain intact. There are, of course, a couple of sports, which are resoundingly blighted by drugs and a lack of integrity, but we needn't go in to that.

As I continued reading the article, the writer claimed that I have more recently become known for coming second, and that my speech at last year's Tournament of Champions was suitably respectful. He probably considered his words complimentary, commenting on my ability to be graceful both in defeat and victory, but I didn't quite see it that way: the 'known for coming second' comment was inaccurate for a start, and unnecessary. Having won some major titles but not with great regularity, it appears I am labelled a 'nearly man'.

It's noticeable that nobody talks about the world No 24 not winning major events. When they say that people are accustomed to my coming second, they forget that everyone from No 5 in the world down is in a similar position, certainly not coming first.

To reach the highest level in anything is deeply challenging. I have spent my life, tens of thousands of hours, doggedly working to become the best. I know how hard it is, and I suppose when journalists, or taxi drivers or the general public, give their opinions without knowing what is fully involved and being comparatively out of their depth, I take it badly.

Andy Murray is a prime example of all this. He is labelled a loser, a perennial runner-up at the time of writing. It is the public's label for him, a compartment in which he is almost made a criminal for not winning. The press refrain from ever calling him a success, even though he has achieved so much at such a young age. Should their own kids have achieved anything similar, their shouting would be heard from every rooftop in London, but merely reaching the finals of Australian and US Opens is deemed a failure.

I know he gets paid well and leads a charmed life, but Murray has to listen to hacks criticising him for seriously challenging three of the greatest tennis players that have ever lived, in Federer, Nadal and Djokovic, and it must be a terrible drain. On the advice of his media team, he continues to say the right things, and desists from biting back.

As a professional squash player, the most criticism I have had has been at times when I have lost to players in a run of matches. People call these players bogey men and it is a good talking point because it suggests a trend, and people love trends. For example, a trend that is mentioned regularly in squash circles is Amr Shabana's inability to win a major tournament in England. He has won every other thing on earth in squash, some events many times, but what do people talk about? Merely the fact that he hasn't won one in England.

It is only due to his incredibly high standard that the question is even asked, but they won't ever settle for a simple answer. The fact that the other player might have simply been better doesn't seem to suffice, instead they prefer to search for a cause – something to do with 'his head' or the weather, or maybe a dislike of English food. My current bogey men, for want of a better phrase, are Ashour and Matthew, against whom I am on substantial losing streaks. The first bogey man I had was Greg Gaultier in the juniors: I probably lost to him 15 times before beating him. But the bogey man to whom people loved to refer the most was former world No 1 Lee Beachill, my training partner for years, who caused me all sorts of problems early in my career.

I lost to Lee countless times before I beat him, while at the same time beating higher-ranked players repeatedly. People questioned what was going on and why I couldn't beat him, suggesting that it was in my head. I reached a point where I became resentful towards the people who asked. The resentment came not from the fact that I wanted to beat Lee, in fact I didn't really think about beating Lee any more than anyone else; I was concerned with a bigger picture, and my main preoccupation was not trying to get one over on my club-mate. People never seemed to give him a great deal of credit either, as if the results were all my doing. His style really stifled my strengths on a squash court and he deserved credit for holding a seemingly unending winning streak for so long.

The bogey man phenomenon is part of sport, but happily there isn't a bogey man that springs to mind which has prevailed eternally, and I am pleased to say that I have overcome mine so far. The problem is that another one may well come along. If life didn't throw up these problems though everything would be incredibly dull.

FOURTEEN

ON THE EDGE
11 February 2011
Sportcity, Manchester. British National Championships
quarter-finals.

I knew when I arrived for a practice at 4pm I was in trouble ahead of my match with Jonathan Kemp: devoid of motivation, I could barely get through 15 minutes of steady hitting. For some reason, being in Manchester and playing in a big tournament seemed like the most unnatural thing on earth. Another competitive match felt wrong. Malc had to listen to me saying that I've had enough of squash, enough of delivering the things for which we have worked so hard and that tactics or effort don't even matter. To me, they didn't at that moment.

I was pathetic and petulant, but he understood. He might have been justified in berating my behaviour but he recognised that I have played, travelled and competed too much at too intense a level in recent months. Burnout.

My physio Alison is a former marathon runner and works mainly in athletics. She maintains that the workload of a squash player is as hard and probably harder than any other sportsman, in terms of the amount of competition undertaken. In 2010 my matches against Nick Matthew in Canary Wharf, David Palmer at the Commonwealth Games, Karim Darwish and Ramy Ashour in Kuwait and not mentioning the two or three consecutive matches at the World Open in Saudi, were all close or over the two-hour mark, almost the equivalent of a marathon, with added twists, turns and joint shattering lunges. This was an unusually tough period, but it is a workload to which we have become accustomed. Alison often compares our schedule to a marathon runner's, and says they wouldn't dream of running five or six marathons in a year and would have four week's rest after each.

Losing 3-1, I felt genuinely happy to be out of the event. At this stage I am too far gone. Perhaps, because of my appetite for achievement, I have lost some of the love of playing that I had as a child. Every match is preceded by build-up and tension, constant thinking and dissecting. The heart races in anticipation and I spend hours wasting energy dealing with nerves. It takes its toll.

I spend the evening with Malc. He asks me if there are any more personal issues involved. He assures me that I won't be able to play and enjoy playing if I am unhappy at home. I'm not sure that's true, and I don't think it's that black and white. I have won matches before on the brink of personal meltdown. I only have to look back at the five in a row winning streak in 2008 for that. Vanessa is on my mind; it becomes clear that I need to address our situation.

As usual I run things over and over in my head all night long. I wonder what it will be like not to live in this world of extremes: misery and joy; action and exhaustion; sleep and insomnia. Perhaps it's the price I pay for caring so much and maybe in that way I am very lucky to have something that drives me.

13 February 2011

Vanessa and I book a hotel in the Yorkshire Dales to purge the events in Manchester. Taking a long walk, we talk as if it is the easiest thing on earth. What have I been so worried and agitated about? I try to consider how my thought process could possibly have become so negative and destructive as it did on Friday against Jonathan.

How do we achieve happiness, and what gives us fulfillment? I think about Mum and wish she was here to offer advice. I think I know what she'd say. During her entire illness she somehow managed to retain great positivity, facing each day on its merit.

I think back to the spring of 2000. Mum was into the second year of her battle against cancer, undergoing regular bouts of chemotherapy. At the time she wasted little energy on the subject of what lay ahead because she couldn't afford to. She was seriously ill, but at the time her condition was sufficiently stable to be exercising and she was playing some squash. She was in fact well enough to enter the club's graded tournament.

She enjoyed herself, won a few games and reached the final. Bald from the chemo, traumatic enough for anyone, let alone a woman who took pride in her appearance, she played the final in front of a packed crowd, donning my 'World Class Performance' baseball cap. How right it was for her to wear that cap: she was the embodiment of beauty, courage and inspiration. I have rarely seen a crowd so engrossed in a club match, and everyone watched as if their lives depended on it. The Saturday night drinkers put aside their glasses, the barmaids stopped serving and even the disinterested friends of friends, who didn't even know her, watched this awe-inspiring display of bravery. She battled her heart out, running for every ball with all of her might and, as the games became close, everyone shouted her name, willing her on to do the unthinkable and win, even though that didn't matter in the slightest.

She lost. Several times I remember being perilously close to bawling my eyes out and I wasn't the only one. It was truly remarkable and I felt unbelievably proud of her. I still keep the trophy at the house we lived in together: 'Runner-up in the Tom Abbot Pontefract Squash Club women's handicap tournament'.

The courage she found, not only that day but every single day of her battle with cancer, is a constant source of inspiration and a valuable example, especially at times like these. Walking in the countryside with Vanessa is exactly how it should be. The future can't be depended upon and it certainly isn't worth worrying about.

Squash is a big part of what I do and who I am but it isn't the be all and end all. I can't allow it to become all-consuming as it sometimes has done in the past. I will take a rest, recover and regain the verve and spirit that has been eaten away. If I can stop worrying about illnesses and injuries, catching colds, agonising over defeats, worrying about the future with Vanessa, and instead concentrate on what can be controlled or what feels best now, then I will be following her example. Let's face it, Mum's battles during those eighteen months were far tougher than any of mine.

So perhaps it is time for me to take a leaf out of Mum's book. No message could be clearer than the one she gave to me that night. When I think back on those fond memories of her, although there is sadness, I feel an overwhelming sense of inspiration and encouragement.

POSTSCRIPT

January 2012

Following his British Nationals defeat, the second half of 2011 proved a revelation for James.

He played for England at the World Team Championships in Germany, where a strong four-man squad finished a disappointing second behind Egypt in a high-tempo final.

A semi-final and final berth in the US and Qatar ensued after which he travelled to Rotterdam for the World Open. With his summer training beginning to pay dividends, he looked in great touch all week but fell to an in-form Gregory Gaultier in the semi-finals at the 1,500-capacity Luxor Theatre. Compatriot Nick Matthew went on to defend his title.

Undeterred, James suddenly found clarity and rhythm to win back-to-back titles at the Hong Kong Open and Kuwait PSA Cup.

November proved to be the best month of his career and James was simply untouchable on court. In those two tournament wins he dropped only one game, at one point winning 28 in a row until Karim Darwish, the loser in both finals to James, scraped one off him in the Kuwait final.

His victories also marked his return to world No 2 for the first time since December 2005. The last time two Englishmen had held the top two spots in the world came in September 2004 when Peter Nicol and Lee Beachill held the same positions.

It didn't stop there. Heading to the PSA Masters in Delhi for the final World Series event of the year, it soon became clear that James would overtake Matthew – who was back in the UK nursing an injury sustained in Kuwait – as world No 1 if he won his third title in a row.

James got through to the final to face career-long rival Gaultier. His inner confidence was evident after losing the first game, which lasted a mere 59 minutes – a record in the modern era of point-a-rally to 11 scoring.

James took the next two games before Gaultier was forced to retire after 99 minutes on court. He'd done it. World No 1 in the January rankings. An incredible end to a year which had started with James questioning both himself and his body.

Could James go one better in 2012 and become world champion?

Rod Gilmour is a sports journalist at *The Daily Telegraph*. He has written on squash since 2008 and will relish the day when the IOC vote the sport onto the Olympic programme.

ACKNOWLEDGEMENTS

Francesca Bullock: thanks for your selfless efforts in promoting the book, and for giving me your advice when decisions needed to be made. Claudia Schurmann: thanks not just for your help with regard to the book, but for your support in general. Steve Bainbridge and Graham Stanford of the SBM group: thank you for seeing value in squash and for committing yourselves to helping me. A thank you also needs to go to Ed Way at Spray Designs. Vanessa: your English Literature studies have helped immensely. Thank you for all your hard work and understanding.